100 Mantras

FOR YOUR HEART & SOUL

Leni Kae

100 Mantras

FOR YOUR HEART & SOUL

Leni Kae

100 Mantras for Your Heart & Soul

First edition published 2025
by Mantra & Stone Co, Australia
www.mantrastone.co | @mantrastone.co

Author Leni Kae
Copyright © 2025 Leni Kae
www.lenikae.com.au | @lenikae

All rights reserved.

No part of this publication may be reproduced, stored in a retrieval system, or transmitted in any form or by any means—electronic, mechanical, photocopying, recording, or otherwise—without prior written consent from Mantra & Stone Co. and Leni Kae. This book is sold subject to the condition that it shall not, by way of trade or otherwise, be resold, lent, hired out, or otherwise circulated without the publisher's prior consent. Any unauthorized acts in relation to this publication may result in civil liability and/or criminal prosecution.

Any content or beliefs shared in this book are intended solely for emotional and spiritual support. This book is not a substitute for professional medical advice, diagnosis, or treatment, nor does it claim to replace guidance from medical professionals or the scientific community.

ISBN: 978-1-7638006-1-8 paperback
ISBN: 978-1-7638006-2-5 e-book

To all the beautiful souls who have ever been brave enough to stand in their own light — thank you. Your courage to follow the whispers of your heart and walk the path of self-discovery is a source of inspiration to this work. This book is for you.

To my precious angel — your presence is a daily reminder of love in its purest form. Your light, laughter, and spirit have been my greatest teachers and my deepest source of inspiration. You remind me what it means to live from the heart.

To my soul team — your connection is a reminder of the power of shared energy and sacred support. Whether near or far, seen or unseen, your light has inspired me. Our connection has been both anchor and wings, and for that, I am endlessly grateful.

~ Leni Kae

**SHARE & TAG YOUR FAVOURITE
MANTRAS ON INSTAGRAM!**

@lenikae

@mantrastone.co

CONTENTS

Introductory Guide ……………….. 9
    What is a Mantra? ………………… 10
    How to Use This Book ……………… 11
        Preparing Your Space and Mind …. 12
        Working With Your Mantra ……… 13

Mantras …………………………….. 15

Notes …………………………….. 117

More …………………………….. 125
    A Gift From the Author ………...126
    About the Author ……….……….. 127
    More Books by Leni Kae ……….129

" Every journey begins with the quiet courage to trust your heart "

– Leni Kae

Introductory Guide

I. WHAT IS A MANTRA?

Mantras are words, phrases, sounds, or chants that centre and focus the mind, increase self-awareness, and invoke energy through intention. This book of 100 mantras offers sacred phrases and poems, divinely inspired through meditation. They may be read silently, spoken, or chanted. You may choose to read them once or repeat them with intention.

The true power of a mantra is achieved when you calmly open and align your primary energy centres with pure intention: the desire in your *heart*, and the will of your *mind*.

Spoken with a mind and heart aligned with good and pure intentions, mantras have the power to shift your perceptions, awaken new feelings, and create new ways of understanding your *Self*.

II. HOW TO USE THIS BOOK

This book has been created for ease of integration into daily life. Simply prepare your space and mind, then open the book intuitively to any page to receive your mantra.

Preparing Your Space & Mind

1. Find a Peaceful Space – Choose a space where you feel calm and at ease. Create a peaceful atmosphere if needed, using soft lighting or gentle music. Sit, stand, or lie down in a comfortable position.
2. Be Aware of your Body - Focus on your body. Starting from your toes and moving up to your facial muscles, can you feel any tension? Relax each muscle one at a time.
3. Relax Your Breathing – Now focus on your breathing. Take a deep breath in, imagine breathing in healing energy and white light. As you breathe out, imagine any residual tension leaving. Then, take slow, comfortable breaths to bring your body to a state of calm and rest.
4. Prepare Your Mind to Receive - While holding the book, set an intention to receive the words you most need today. For example, you might think or softly speak the words:

"I will receive the words that my heart and soul need today"
or
"Reveal a mantra to align my heart and soul"

Working With Your Mantra

1. Intuitively Open the Book to Any Page
2. Read Your Mantra – As you read your mantra, allow your mind to focus on the words. Notice how they come together to form meaning and intention. Pay attention to any symbolism the words may hold. Feel them with your heart, and be aware of any emotions they stir, memories they awaken, or visuals you receive.
3. Take Notes – You may choose to write down any feelings, insights, or lessons in the Notes section at the end of this book to refer to later.
4. Close with Gratitude – To complete, thank your consciousness and higher self for any learnings and awakenings experienced.

" With every breath,
there is opportunity
to grow "

– Leni Kae

*" Make every mantra
a heartfelt prayer
to your Soul "*

– Leni Kae

Mantras

1

I live each day
to honour my heart

2

I choose
in this moment
to awaken with new spirit
~ the spirit of new perspective ~

I will create my rainbow
its Truth I will embrace
I will swim in all its colours
with glory and good grace

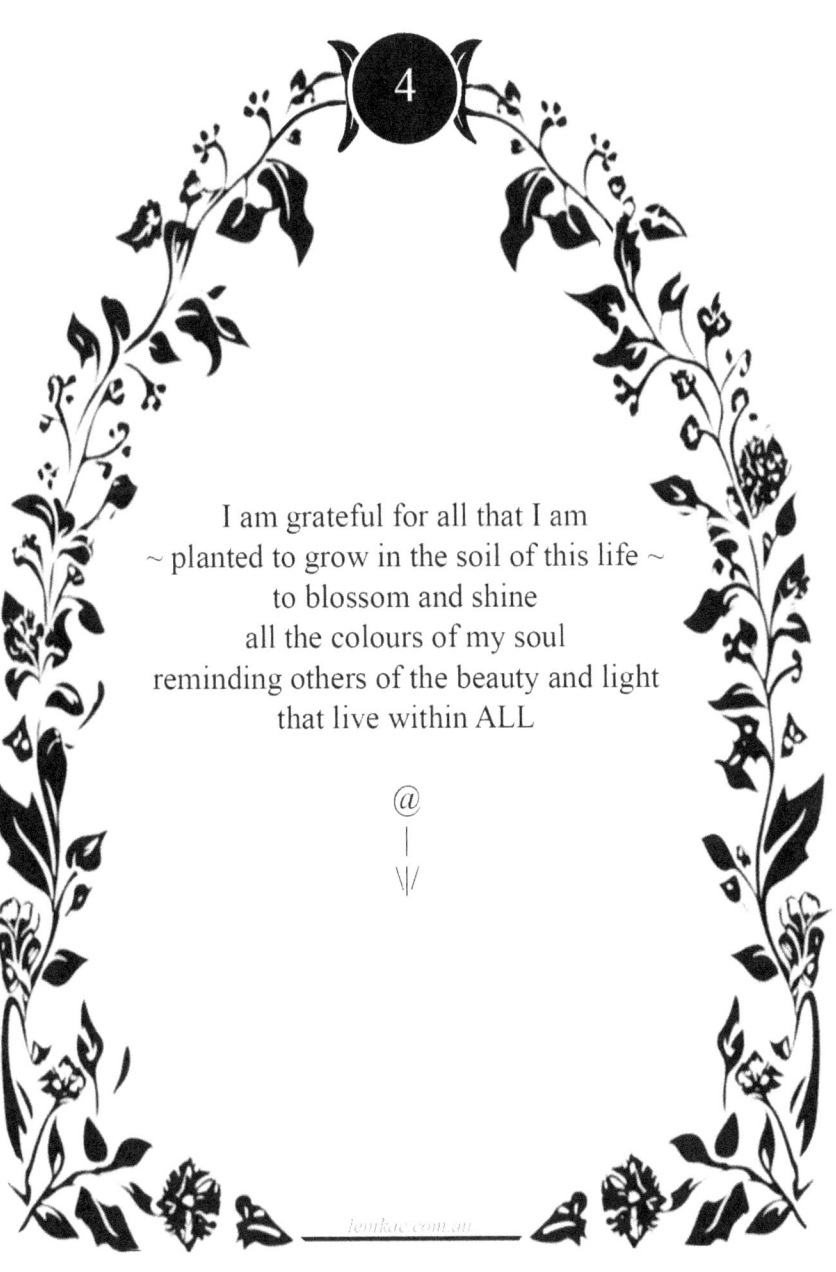

4

I am grateful for all that I am
~ planted to grow in the soil of this life ~
to blossom and shine
all the colours of my soul
reminding others of the beauty and light
that live within ALL

5

I am grateful
for the small things
~ for the glimmers of beauty ~
that bring my heart into
peace
wonder
joy

.
/|\

I honour the calling
of my soul's highest Truth
I allow this Truth to flow through me
honest and unfiltered
guiding me towards my joy

7

I trust
in the Divine love
and timeless bonds
of my soul family tree —
connected with one another
in life and in spirit
drawn to one another
in perfect timing —
to align
to grow
to rise
together

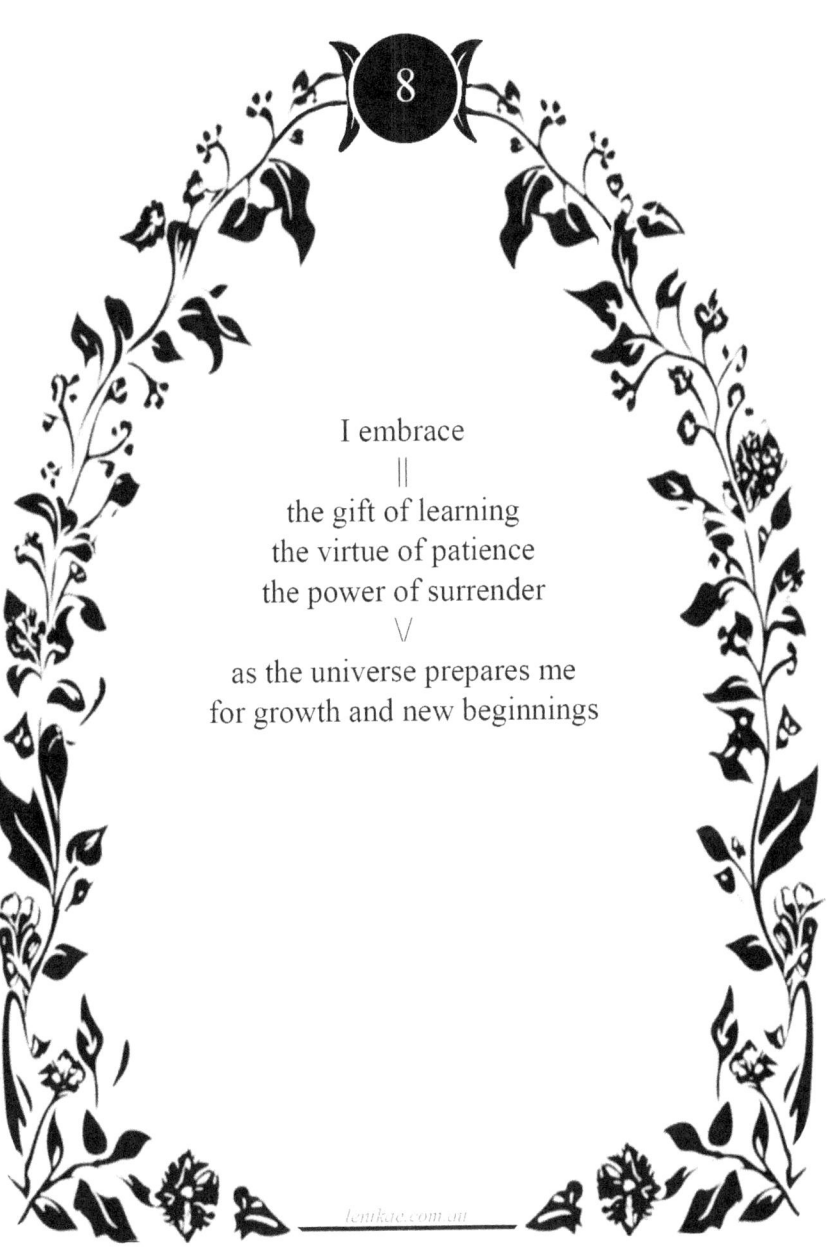

I embrace
||
the gift of learning
the virtue of patience
the power of surrender
\/
as the universe prepares me
for growth and new beginnings

I choose
every day
to treat myself
with love, patience, kindness
\|/
/|\
embodying the energy
that I wish
to attract

I embrace this moment
with nature as my guide
affirming my connection
to Mother Earth
to renewal and rebirth
to my daily opportuniy
to grow and flourish
\|/
into a new me

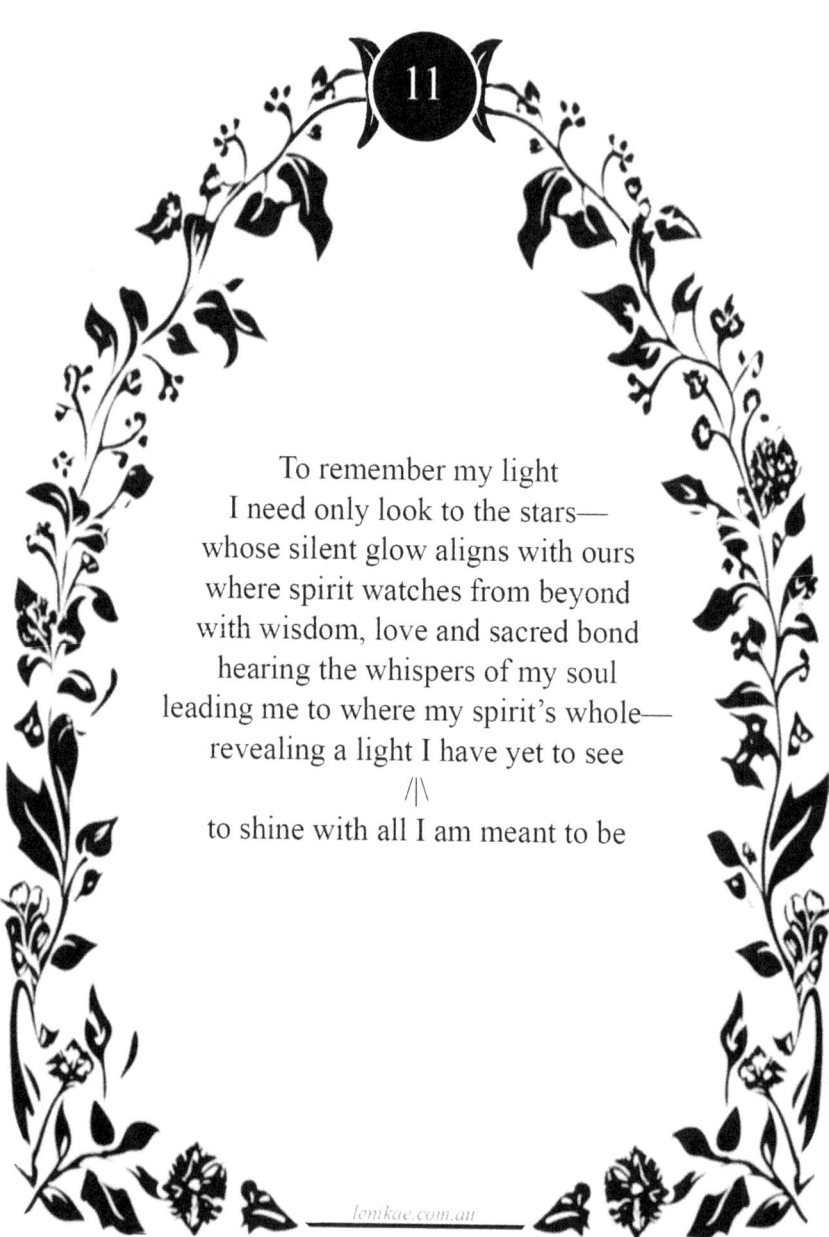

11

To remember my light
I need only look to the stars—
whose silent glow aligns with ours
where spirit watches from beyond
with wisdom, love and sacred bond
hearing the whispers of my soul
leading me to where my spirit's whole—
revealing a light I have yet to see
/|\
to shine with all I am meant to be

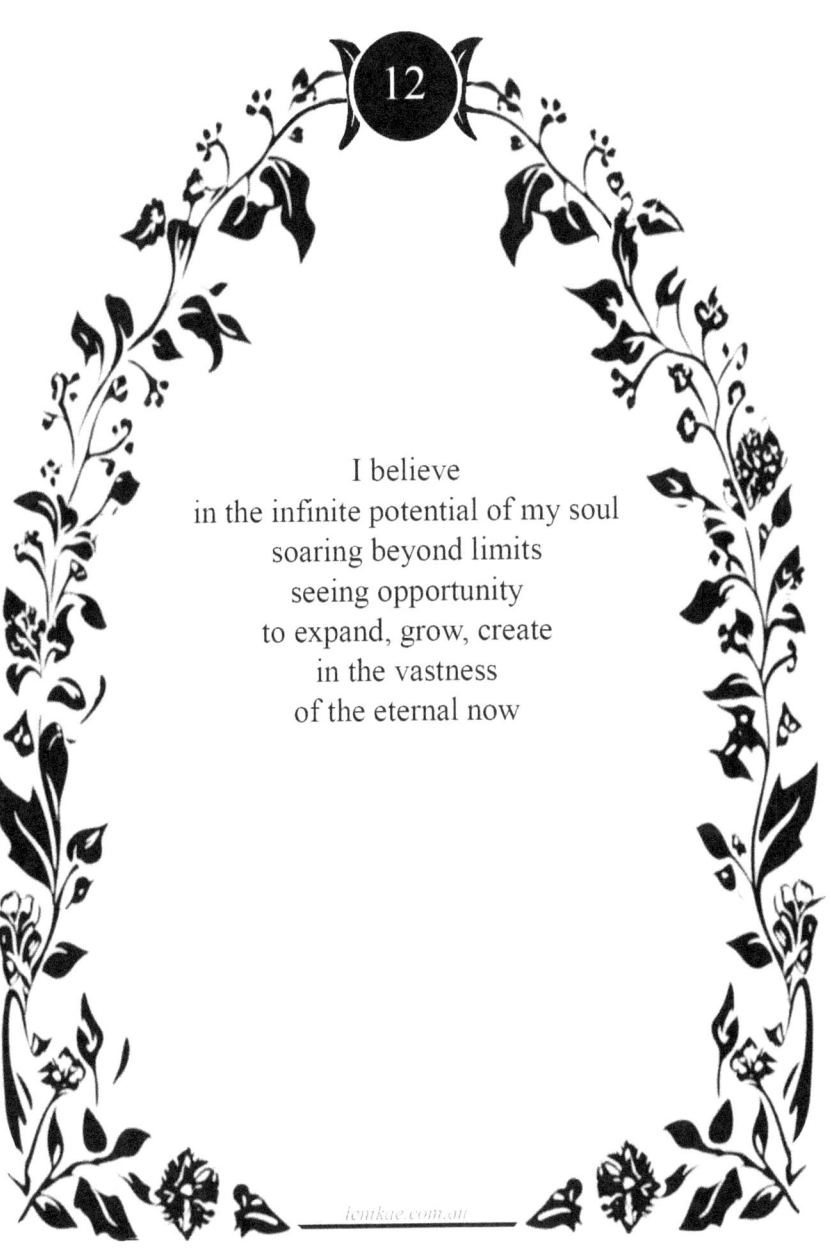

12

I believe
in the infinite potential of my soul
soaring beyond limits
seeing opportunity
to expand, grow, create
in the vastness
of the eternal now

13

I believe
in the light that flows through ALL
weaving us together
into an infinite tapestry of
connected light and love

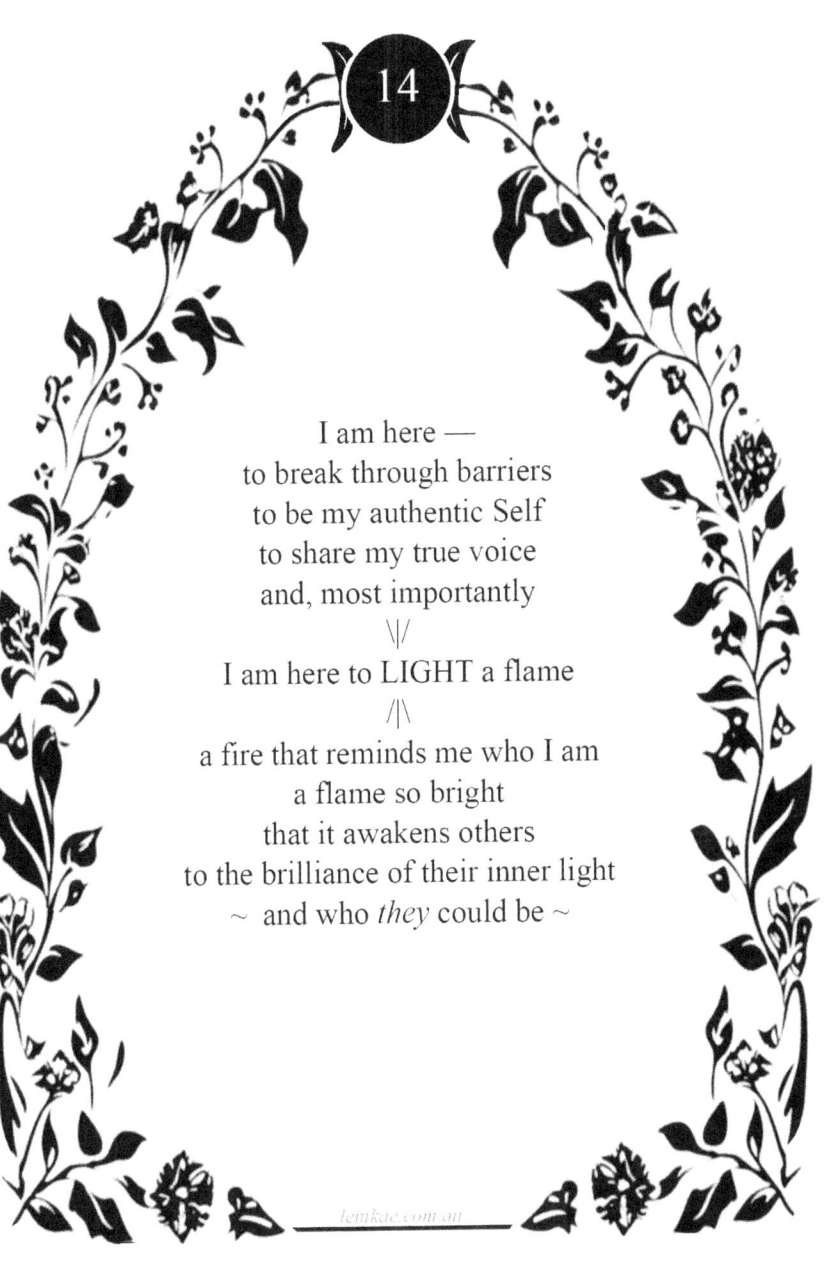

I am here —
to break through barriers
to be my authentic Self
to share my true voice
and, most importantly
\|/
I am here to LIGHT a flame
/|\
a fire that reminds me who I am
a flame so bright
that it awakens others
to the brilliance of their inner light
~ and who *they* could be ~

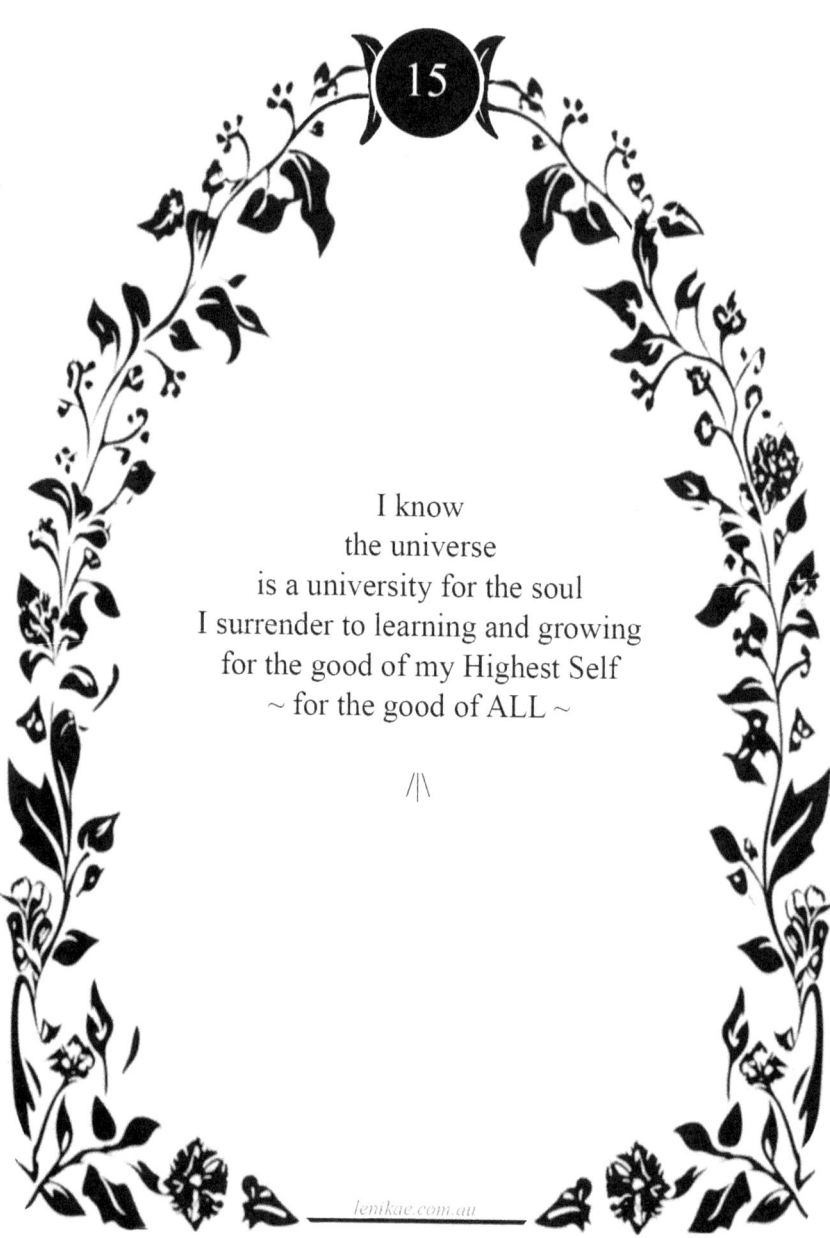

15

I know
the universe
is a university for the soul
I surrender to learning and growing
for the good of my Highest Self
~ for the good of ALL ~

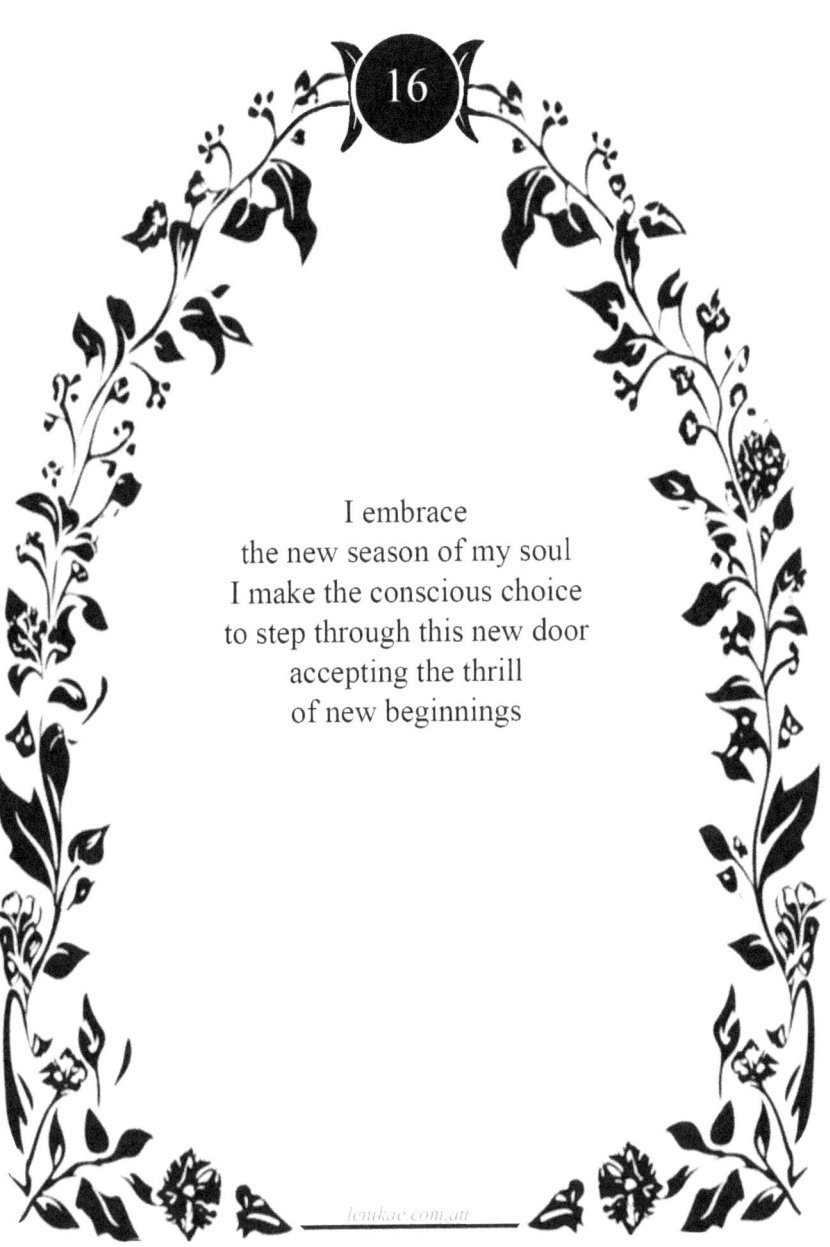

16

I embrace
the new season of my soul
I make the conscious choice
to step through this new door
accepting the thrill
of new beginnings

17

I believe
in the light
of my eternal flame
enlightening my soul
to shadows and truths
as I find my way home
to the Truth
of who I am

18

I surrender
to the flow of the universe
trusting the Divine current
to guide the journey of my soul

I nurture
the fire of my soul
feeding the flames of passion
that set my heart
alight

In this moment
I am loved
I am safe
I am protected

./|\

I trust in the power of Divine Light
to cleanse and protect me
within and without

21

I embrace
the stillness within
for in my silence
I can better hear
the guiding whispers
of my soul

22

I dance
with the cleansing winds of change
I embrace the Divine beauty
of fresh beginnings
~ new light, love and wisdom ~
that will come my way

23

I release the weight
of what no longer serves

I embrace the peace
that my soul deserves

24

I trust the rhythm
of my heart's sacred streams

I flow with faith
towards my wildest dreams

25

I speak
with the voice of my soul
carrying messages of Truth
wherever I go

26

Like a phoenix in flames
from the ashes I rise
with fire in my heart
burning bright in my eyes
I reclaim my power
I stand in my strength
I am limitless, empowered
soaring high without end

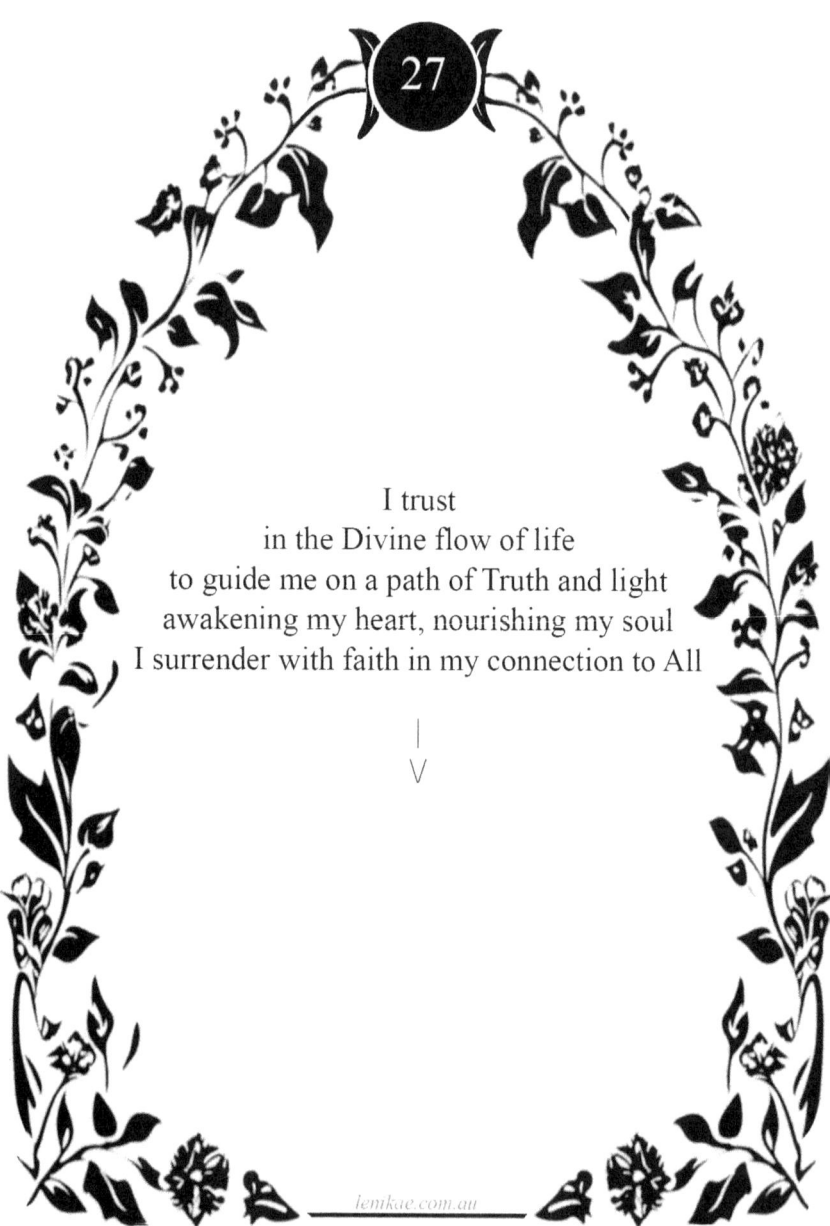

27

I trust
in the Divine flow of life
to guide me on a path of Truth and light
awakening my heart, nourishing my soul
I surrender with faith in my connection to All

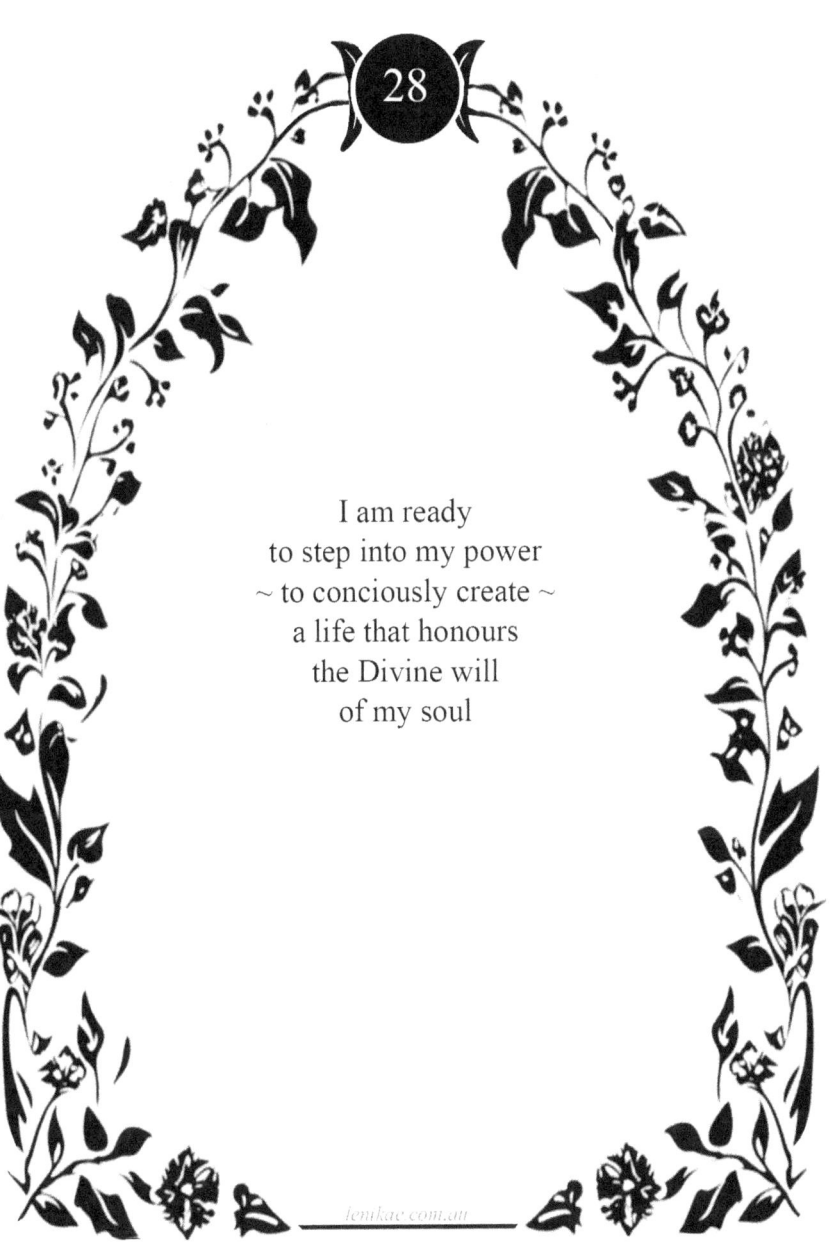

I am ready
to step into my power
~ to conciously create ~
a life that honours
the Divine will
of my soul

29

I see the Divine spark
within all living beings
for we are all connected
in life, with love
to the same Divine light
here and above

30

I embody
the will of my highest Self

...

\|/

I trust
in the Divine purpose
chosen for this expression
of my soul

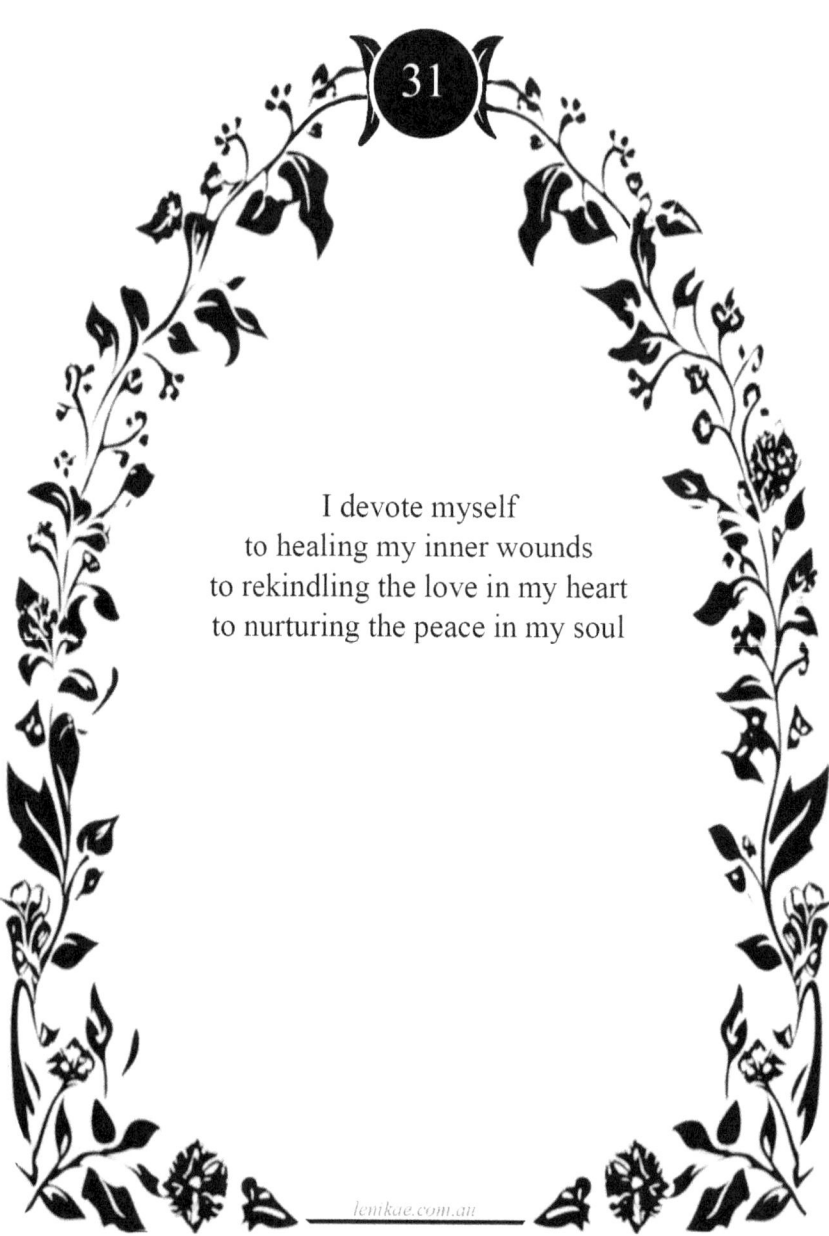

I devote myself
to healing my inner wounds
to rekindling the love in my heart
to nurturing the peace in my soul

32

I awaken
the Divine wisdom of my ancestors
carried by my vessel
embedded within my soul

O
+
\/

33

I am worthy
of Divine Love
~ the sacred energy ~
flowing through my heart
illuminating my soul

34

I awaken
the Divine courage
to walk my sacred path
guided by the fire of my purpose
to fulfil the will of my highest good

/\
|
|
\/

I awaken
to the beauty in small things
the pleasure found in sacred moments
of peace, joy, connection

36

I embrace my magic
as a conscious creator
of my world

/\
o
\/

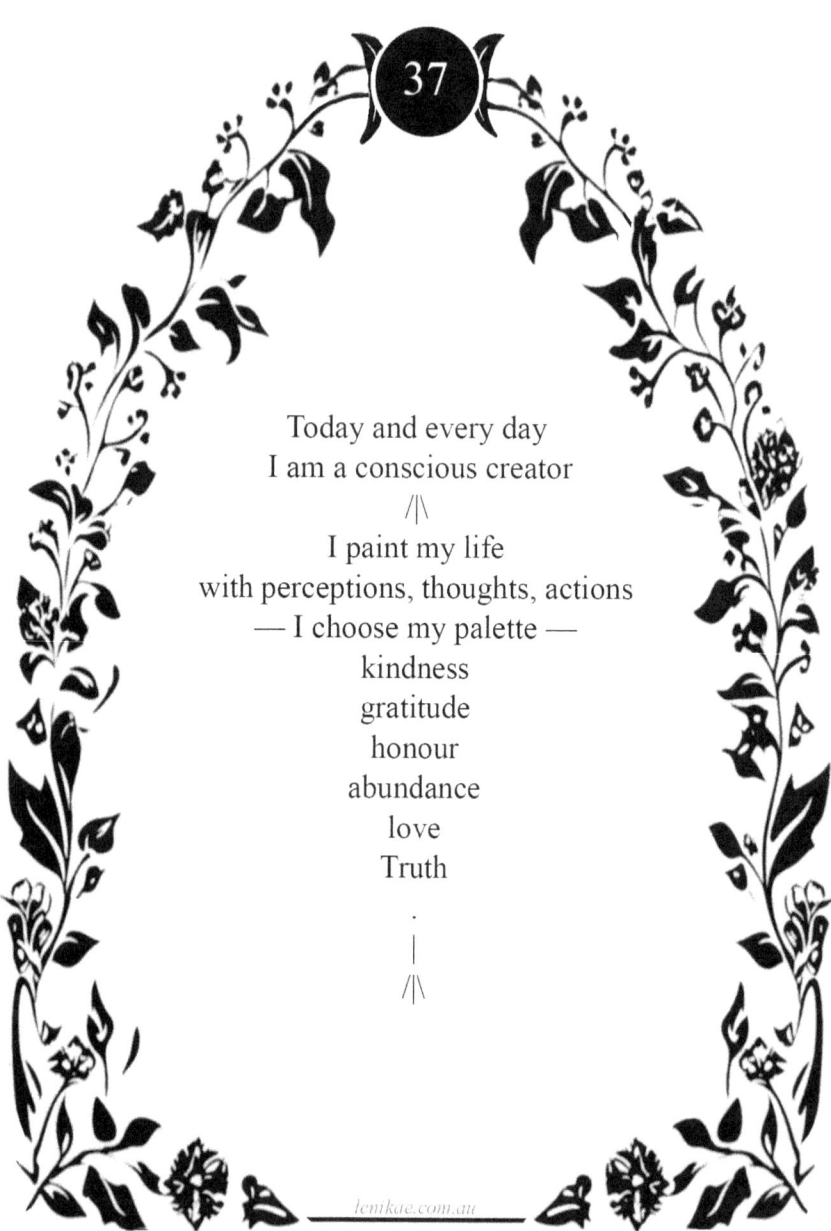

Today and every day
I am a conscious creator
/|\
I paint my life
with perceptions, thoughts, actions
— I choose my palette —
kindness
gratitude
honour
abundance
love
Truth

.
|
/|\

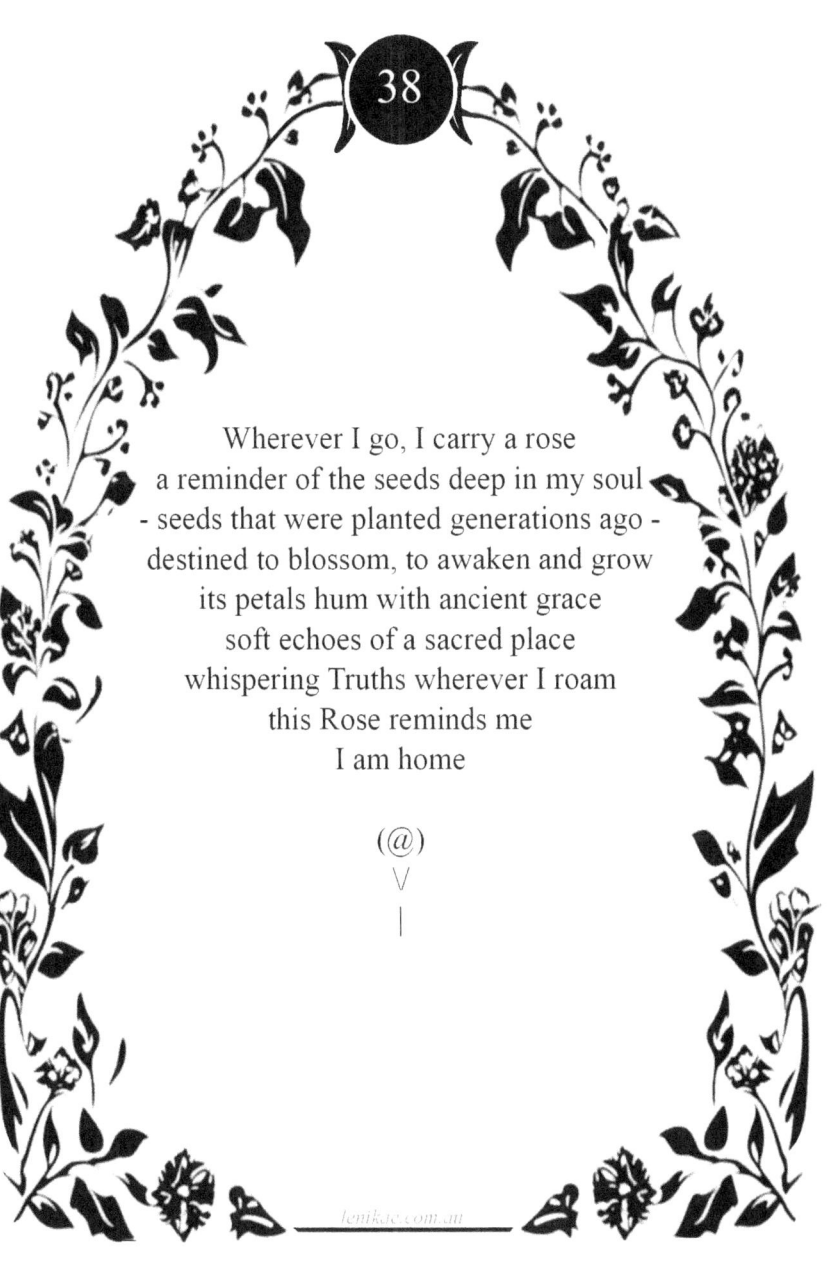

38

Wherever I go, I carry a rose
a reminder of the seeds deep in my soul
- seeds that were planted generations ago -
destined to blossom, to awaken and grow
its petals hum with ancient grace
soft echoes of a sacred place
whispering Truths wherever I roam
this Rose reminds me
I am home

(@)
\/
|

39

I embrace
the sacred gift
of the present moment

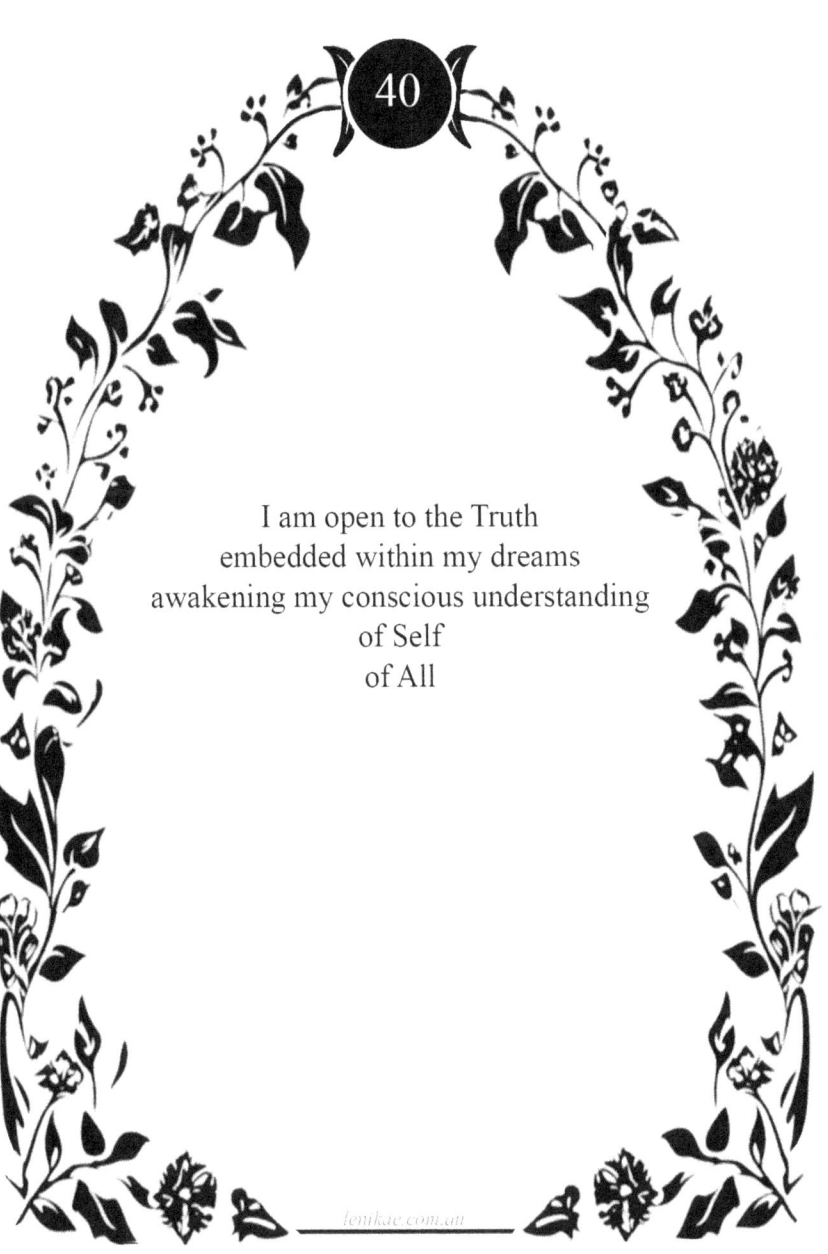

40

I am open to the Truth
embedded within my dreams
awakening my conscious understanding
of Self
of All

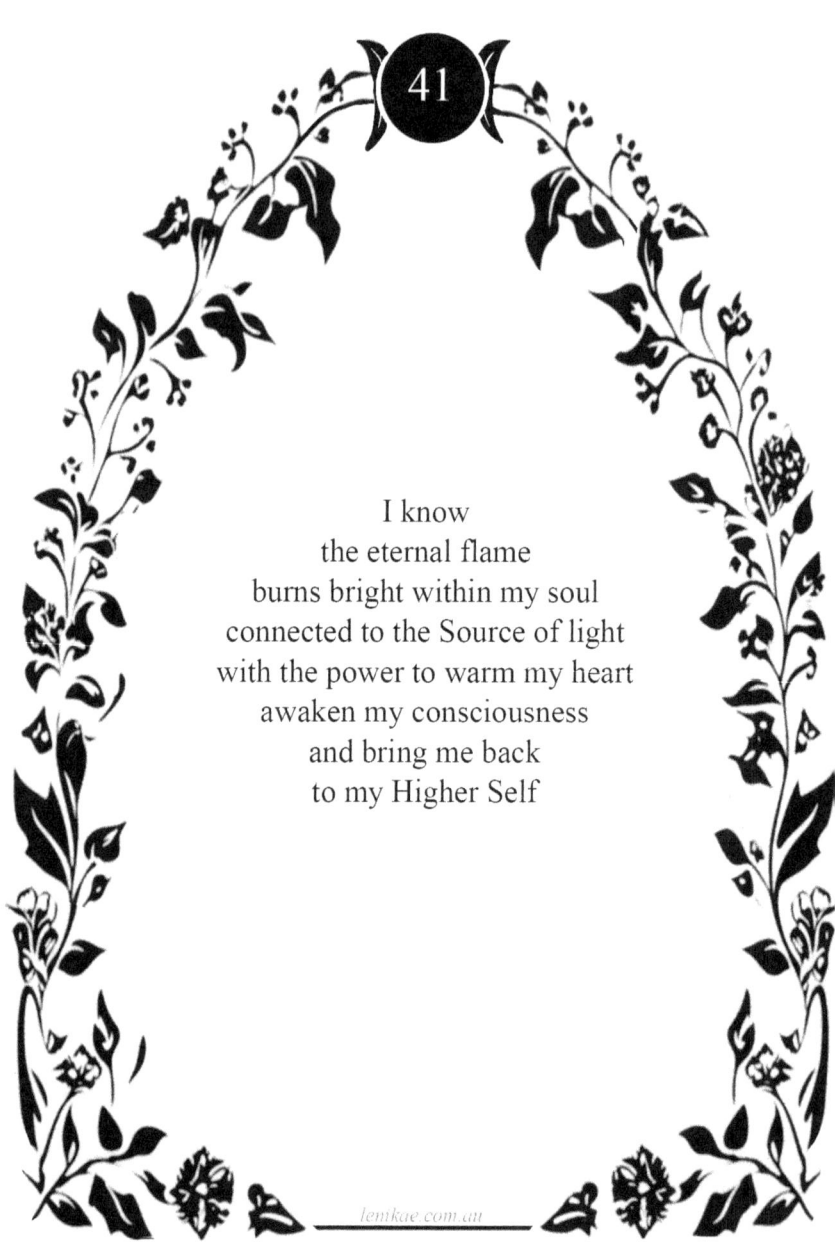

41

I know
the eternal flame
burns bright within my soul
connected to the Source of light
with the power to warm my heart
awaken my consciousness
and bring me back
to my Higher Self

42

Within my heart is a bird
ready to spread its wings
to fly high and soar
with love and new persepctive

43

I give thanks to the Rose
whose petals unfold, whose beauty blooms
awakening with the elements, never to soon
carrying a message of Truth in its sacred design
~ all will blossom in Divine time ~

((.))
|

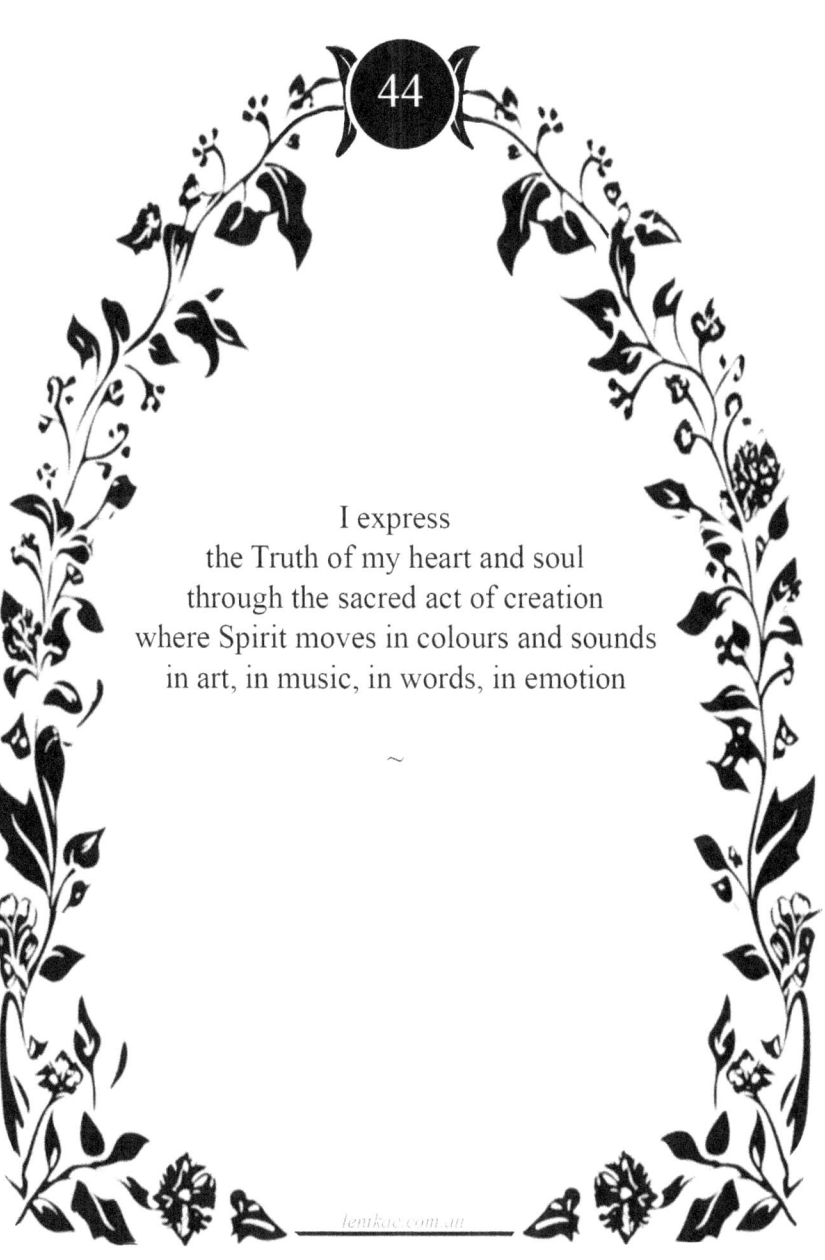

44

I express
the Truth of my heart and soul
through the sacred act of creation
where Spirit moves in colours and sounds
in art, in music, in words, in emotion

~

45

I am grateful
to the sacred animal Spirits
of earth, sky and sea
who find me in moments of need
bearing gifts of silent wisdom
of companionship and unconditonal love
of Divine primal energy
to awaken my senses
to heal my heart
to enlighten my soul

lenikae.com.au

46

All is my mirror, clear and true
a reflection of what I must journey through
revealing my shadows, reflecting my light
I am ready and willing, I open my eyes
I see, I learn, I shed
I rise

47

I am protected
enveloped in a golden glow
in light that flows from Source to soul

48

I trust the sacred rhythm of the Divine
I surrender to life's grand design
In stillness and grace, all Truths align

|

What is meant for me shall be mine

V

I welcome
the wisdom woven into every moment
with each experience, a teacher
guiding me toward my highest light

50

I make this sacred promise to my soul
/|||\
to embrace each experience
as an oppportunity to learn
to act with love
to rise with grace
to grow in ever-deepening alignment
with my Truest self

51

I trust
in the flow
of the ocean of life

~~~

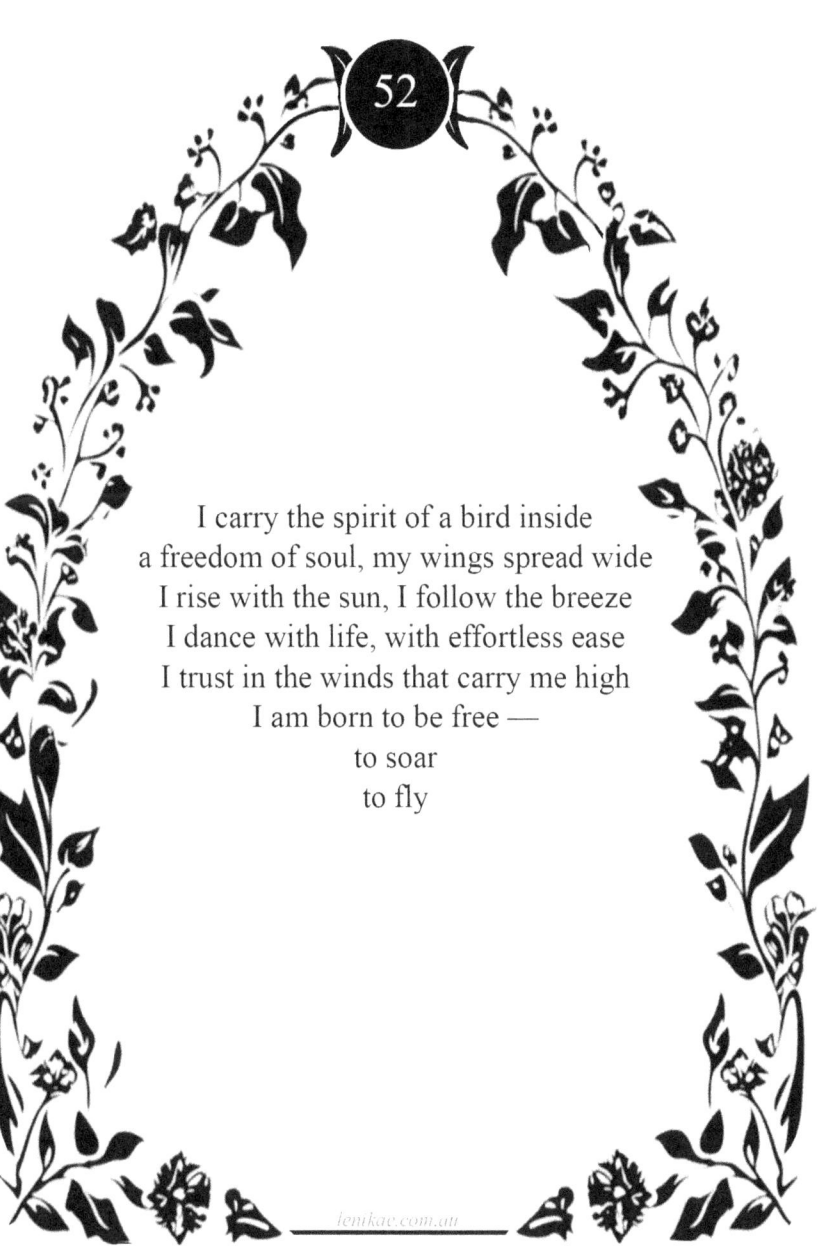

I carry the spirit of a bird inside
a freedom of soul, my wings spread wide
I rise with the sun, I follow the breeze
I dance with life, with effortless ease
I trust in the winds that carry me high
I am born to be free —
to soar
to fly

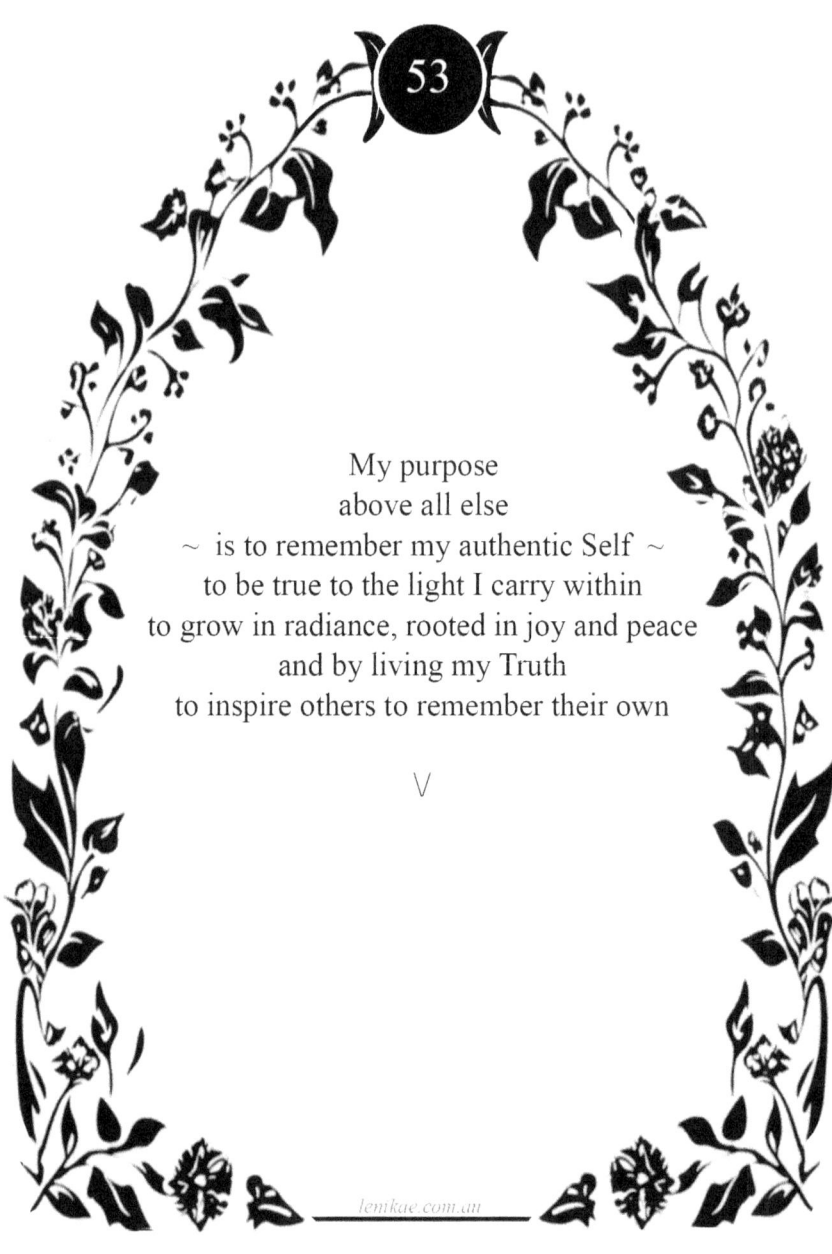

53

My purpose
above all else
~ is to remember my authentic Self ~
to be true to the light I carry within
to grow in radiance, rooted in joy and peace
and by living my Truth
to inspire others to remember their own

V

lenikae.com.au

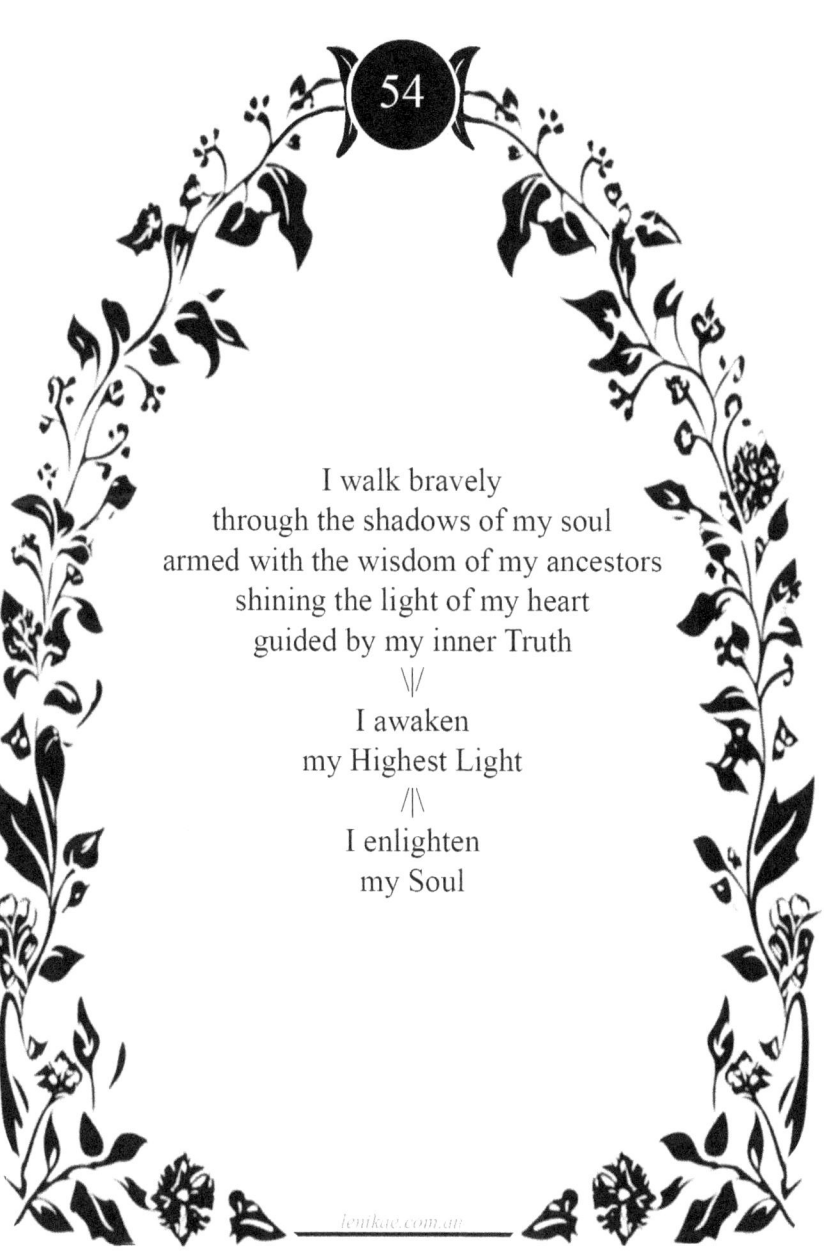

54

I walk bravely
through the shadows of my soul
armed with the wisdom of my ancestors
shining the light of my heart
guided by my inner Truth
\|/
I awaken
my Highest Light
/|\
I enlighten
my Soul

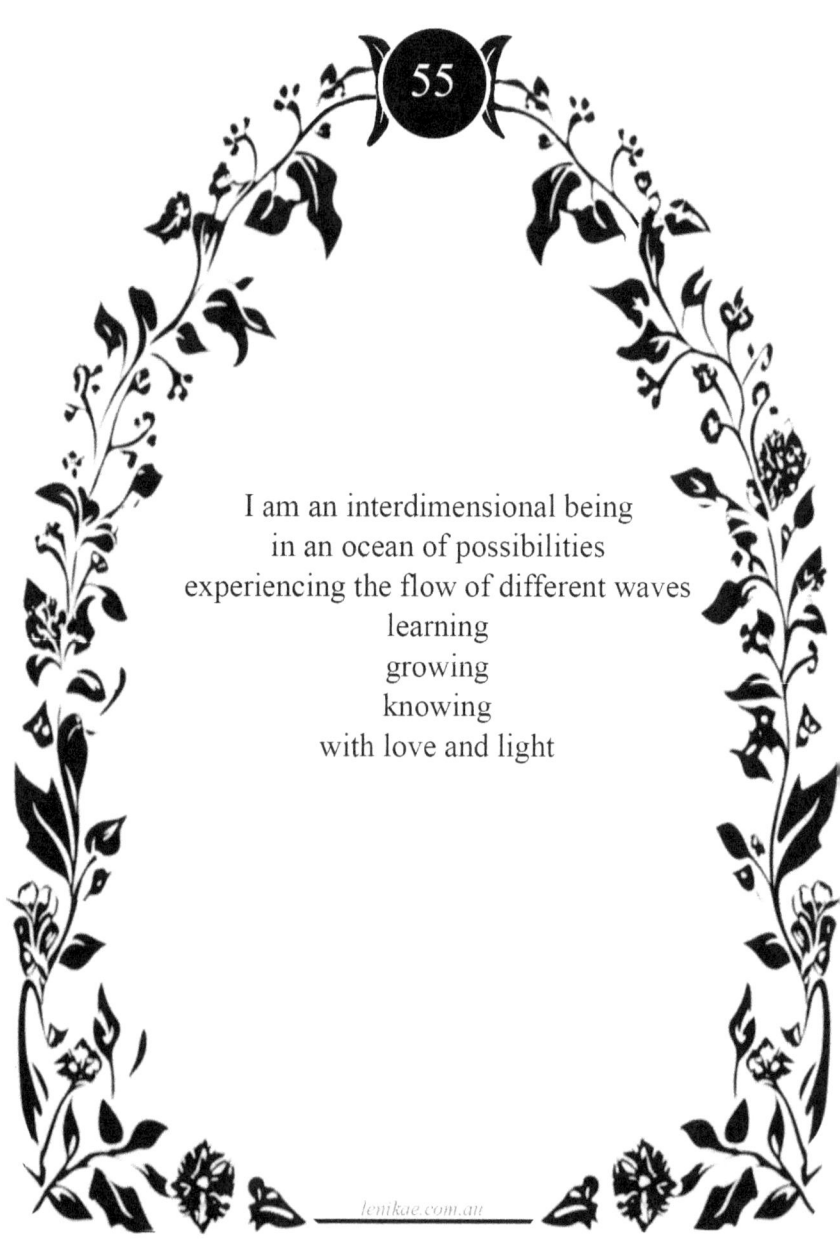

55

I am an interdimensional being
in an ocean of possibilities
experiencing the flow of different waves
learning
growing
knowing
with love and light

56

I am connected to the stars above
through stardust threads of light and love
Across the skies, my dreams take flight
their song embraced by cosmic light

57

With warmth and grace, soft and true
through love and light in all I do
my heart unfolds its petals slow
a rose in bloom, with sacred glow

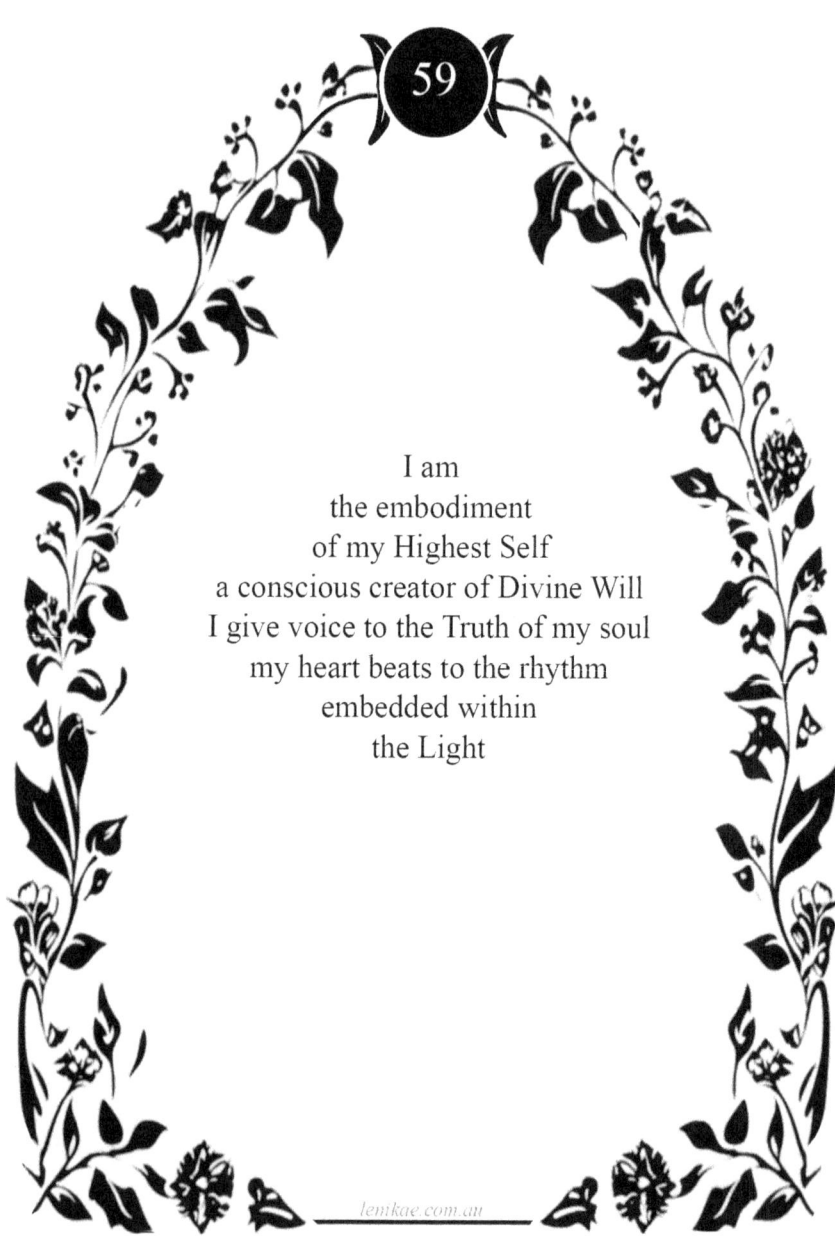

I am
the embodiment
of my Highest Self
a conscious creator of Divine Will
I give voice to the Truth of my soul
my heart beats to the rhythm
embedded within
the Light

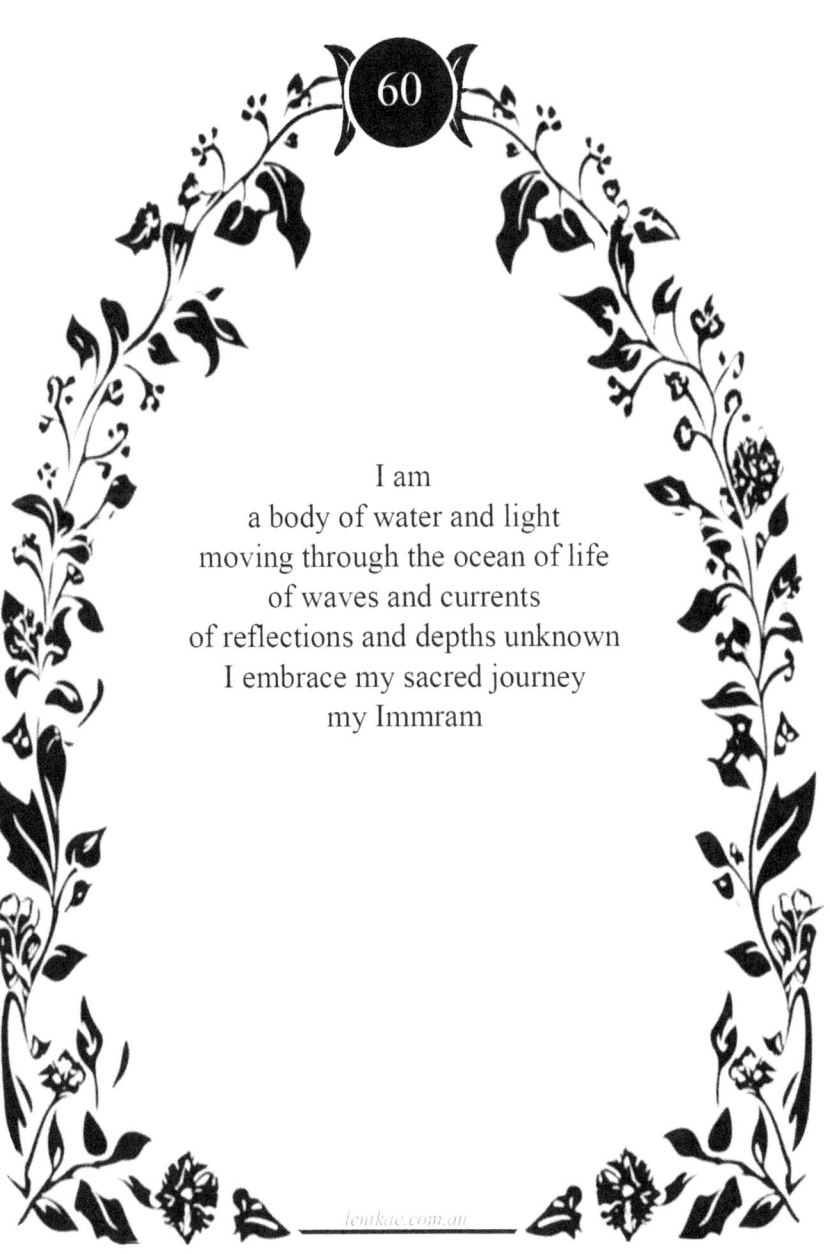

60

I am
a body of water and light
moving through the ocean of life
of waves and currents
of reflections and depths unknown
I embrace my sacred journey
my Immram

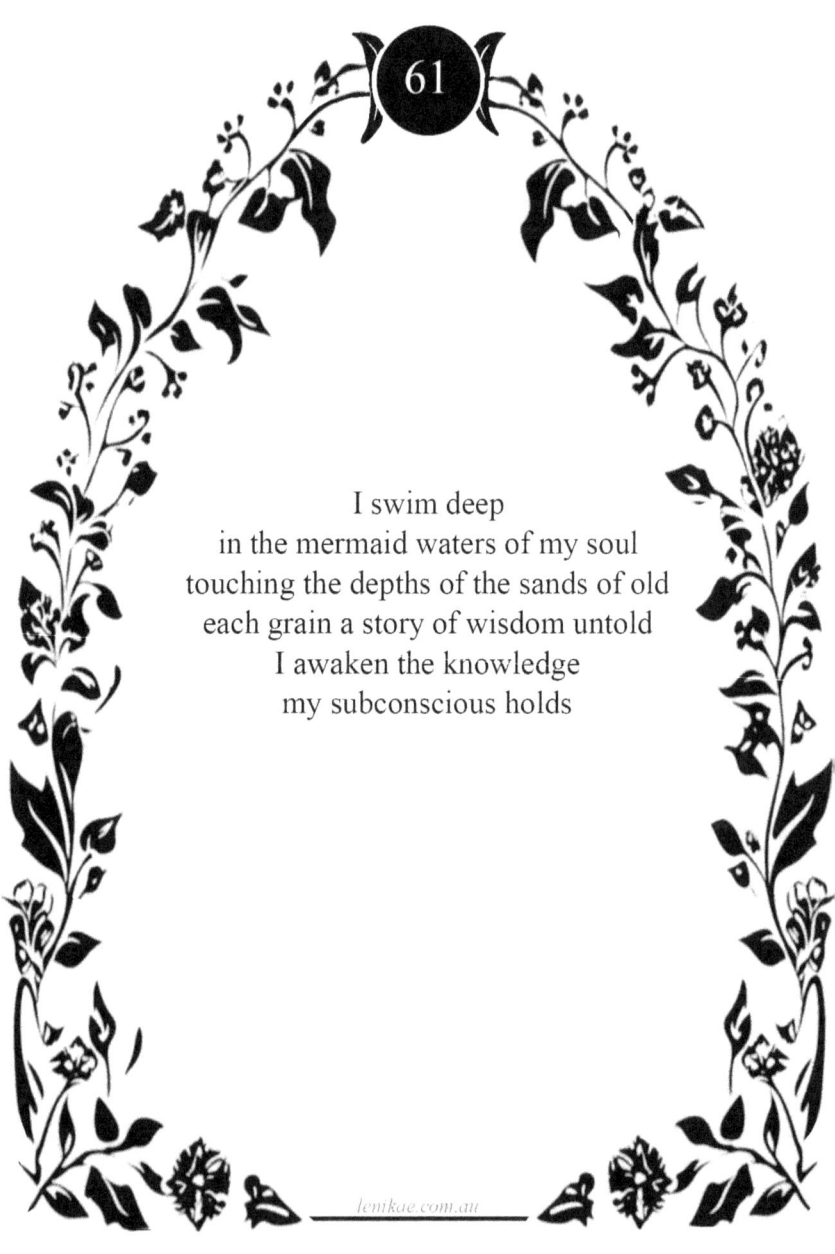

I swim deep
in the mermaid waters of my soul
touching the depths of the sands of old
each grain a story of wisdom untold
I awaken the knowledge
my subconscious holds

62

I awaken
lucid in this dream of life
ready to embody my vision
of joy, love, abundance

63

I dance freely
to the music of my soul

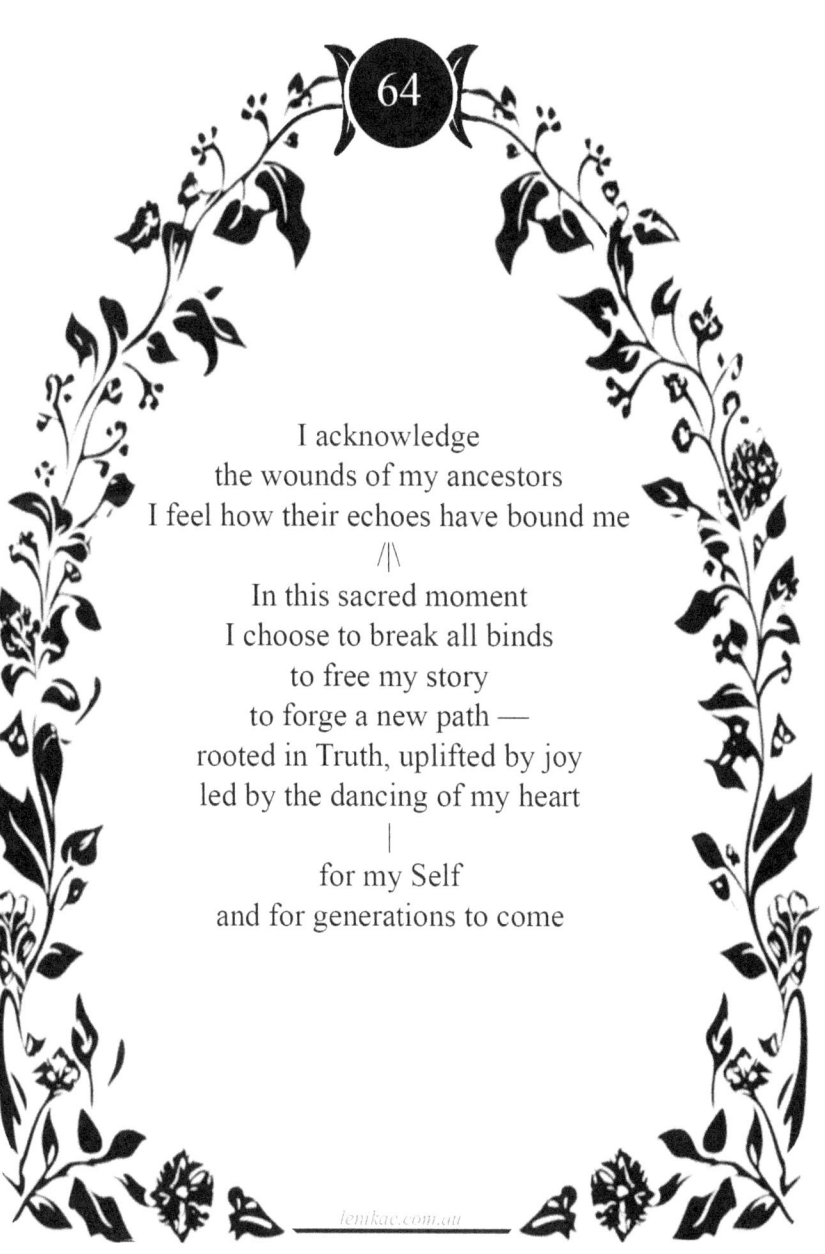

64

I acknowledge
the wounds of my ancestors
I feel how their echoes have bound me
/|\
In this sacred moment
I choose to break all binds
to free my story
to forge a new path —
rooted in Truth, uplifted by joy
led by the dancing of my heart
|
for my Self
and for generations to come

65

~ I choose to love ~
for to love is to awaken
the sacred essence of my soul
my heart's connection to the stars of old
~ I open to love in all its forms ~
for Self, for others, for nature, for life
in love, I breathe, I shine, I rise
/|\

in love, my soul remembers its light

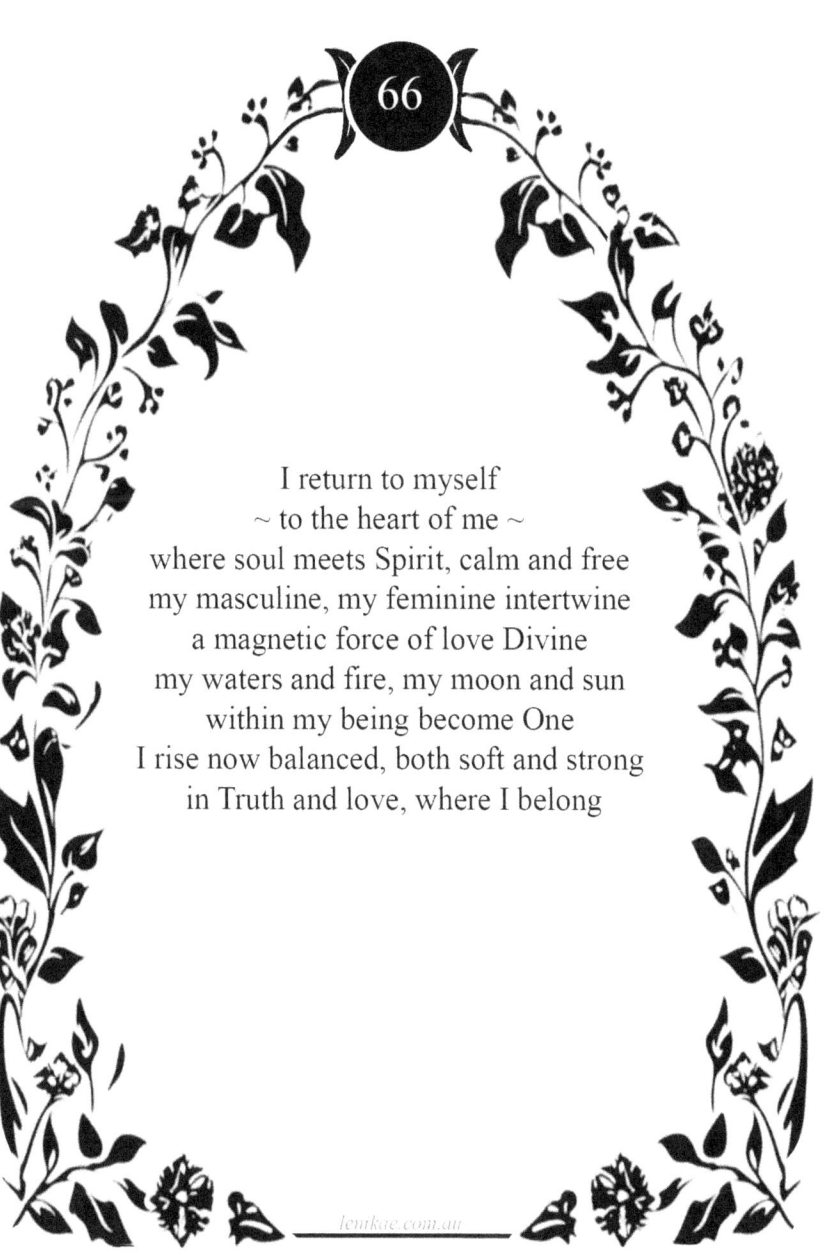

66

I return to myself
~ to the heart of me ~
where soul meets Spirit, calm and free
my masculine, my feminine intertwine
a magnetic force of love Divine
my waters and fire, my moon and sun
within my being become One
I rise now balanced, both soft and strong
in Truth and love, where I belong

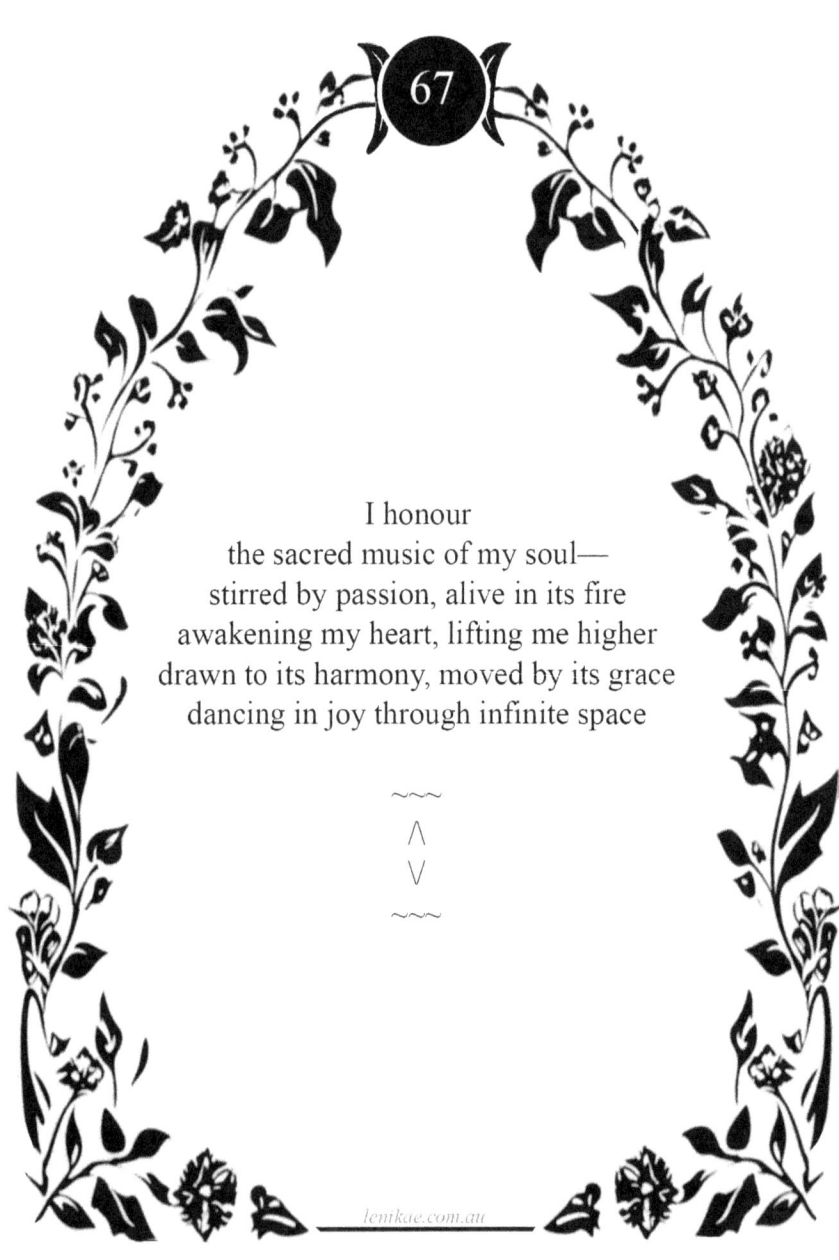

67

I honour
the sacred music of my soul—
stirred by passion, alive in its fire
awakening my heart, lifting me higher
drawn to its harmony, moved by its grace
dancing in joy through infinite space

68

I follow what makes my heart sing
I nourish my flame, my light within
In truth, in peace, I now align—
This life, this love, this light is mine

69

I cleanse the sacred waters
of my body and soul
within, without
above, below
I see with clarity
I move with flow

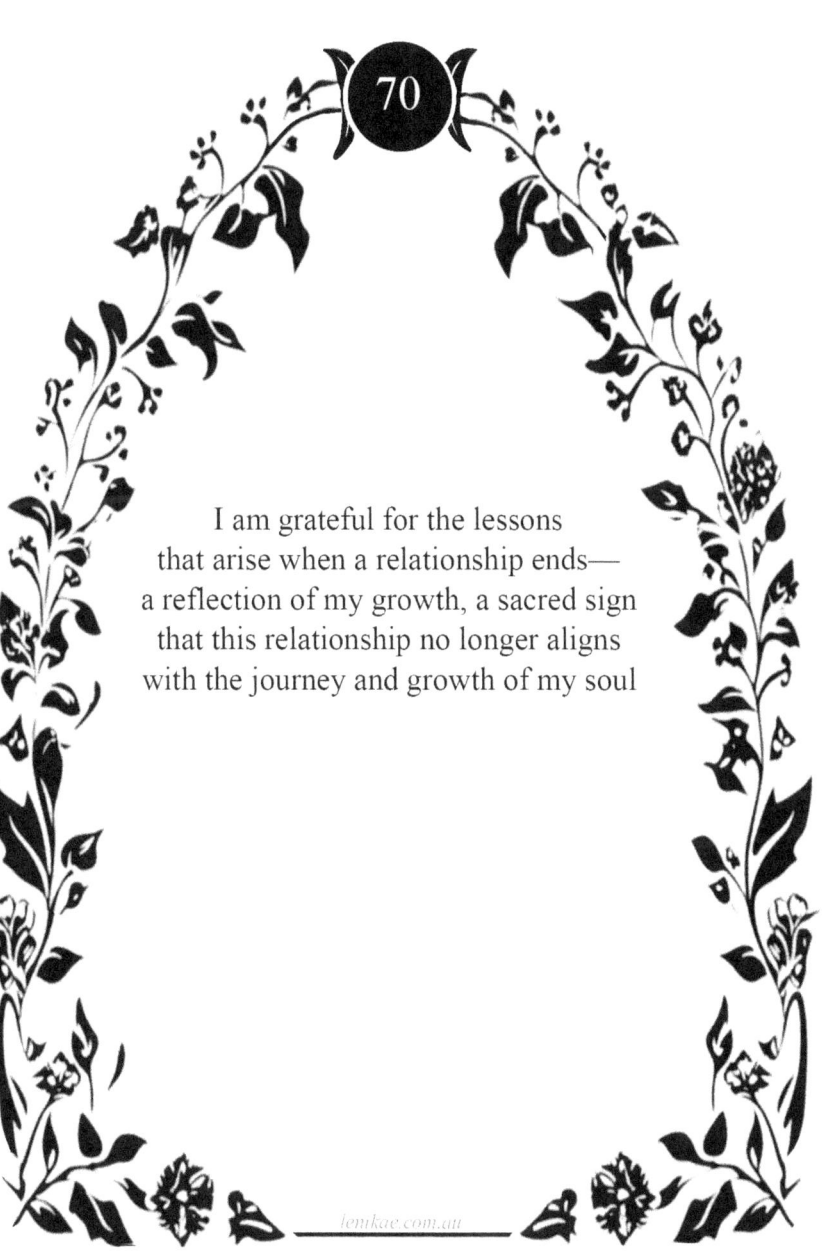

70

I am grateful for the lessons
that arise when a relationship ends—
a reflection of my growth, a sacred sign
that this relationship no longer aligns
with the journey and growth of my soul

71

With each ending
I witness my growth
I feel what no longer brings me joy
I see with clarity the choices before me
I learn the sacred strength of boundaries
I acknowledge my worth and all I deserve
and so, I affirm—

||

I am ready for more

||
/ \

72

I ground my energy
from the core of my being
to the center of the Earth
bonded in spirit through the fire in my heart
connected in body, anchored in soil—
I stand strong, rooted in body and soul

73

From my light above
to my light on earth
I deserve abundance
I know my worth

74

I align my energy
from above to below
through my heart's centre
may Divine light flow

I repel
the negative emotions of others
seeing them as reflections of *their* wounds
their trauma, conditioning
their unfulfilled dreams
or what *they* lack

―――

||

―――

I choose
to remain anchored in positivity
enveloped in the Divine love and light
of my Truth

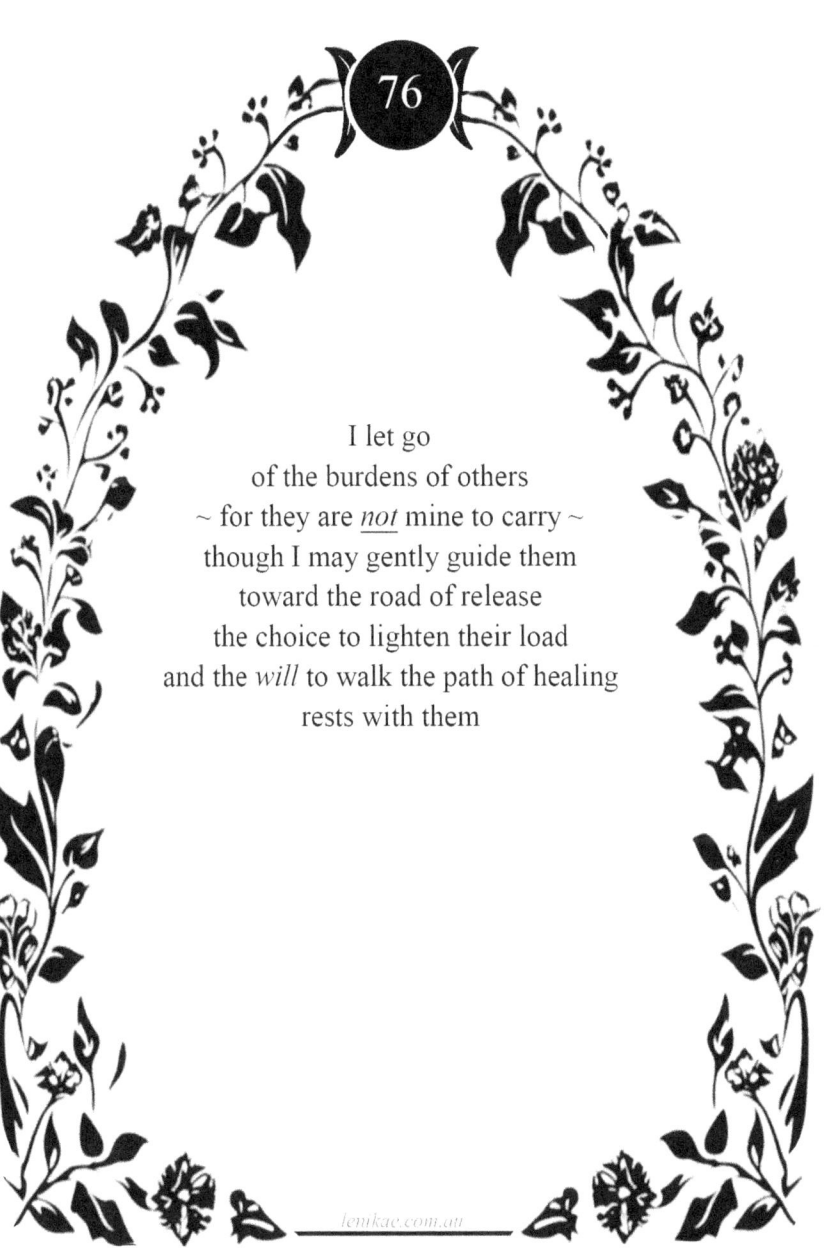

76

I let go
of the burdens of others
~ for they are *not* mine to carry ~
though I may gently guide them
toward the road of release
the choice to lighten their load
and the *will* to walk the path of healing
rests with them

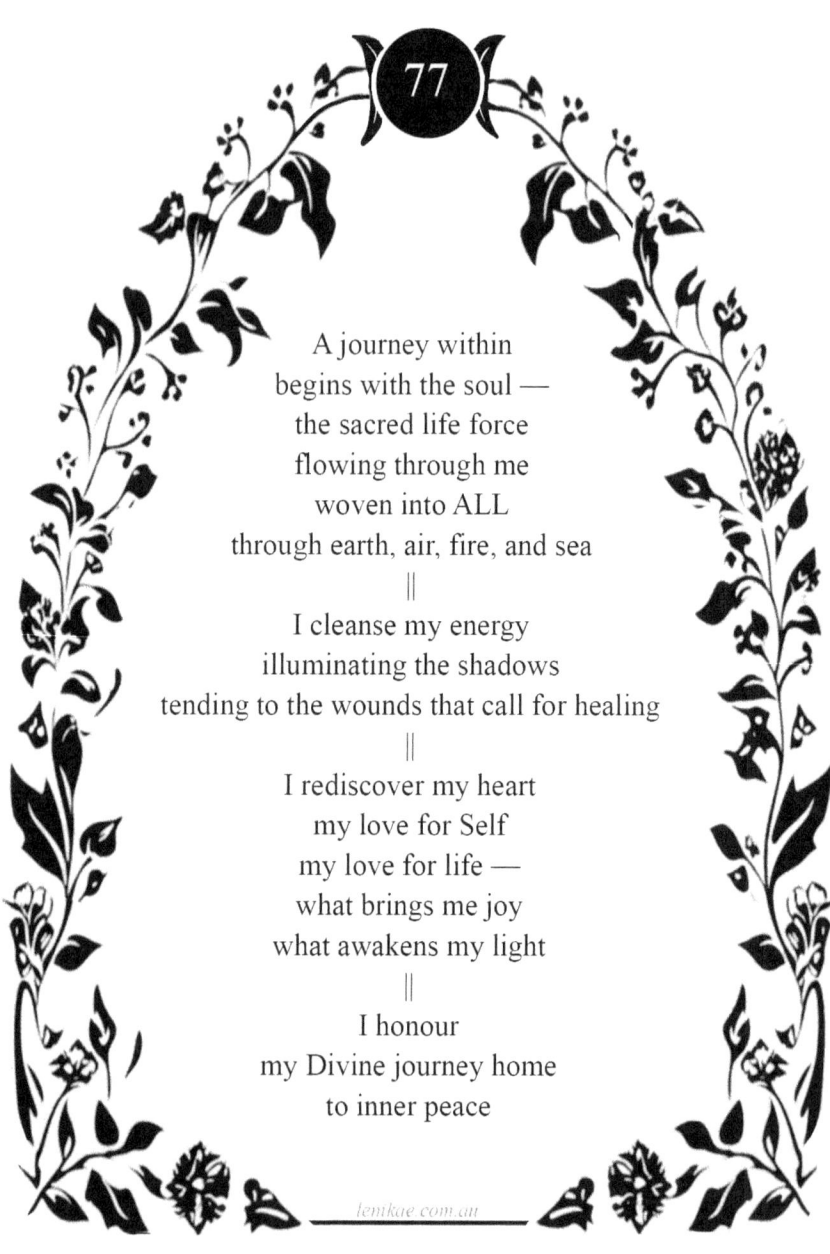

77

A journey within
begins with the soul —
the sacred life force
flowing through me
woven into ALL
through earth, air, fire, and sea

||

I cleanse my energy
illuminating the shadows
tending to the wounds that call for healing

||

I rediscover my heart
my love for Self
my love for life —
what brings me joy
what awakens my light

||

I honour
my Divine journey home
to inner peace

78

In love and light
I honour what delights
my heart, my soul

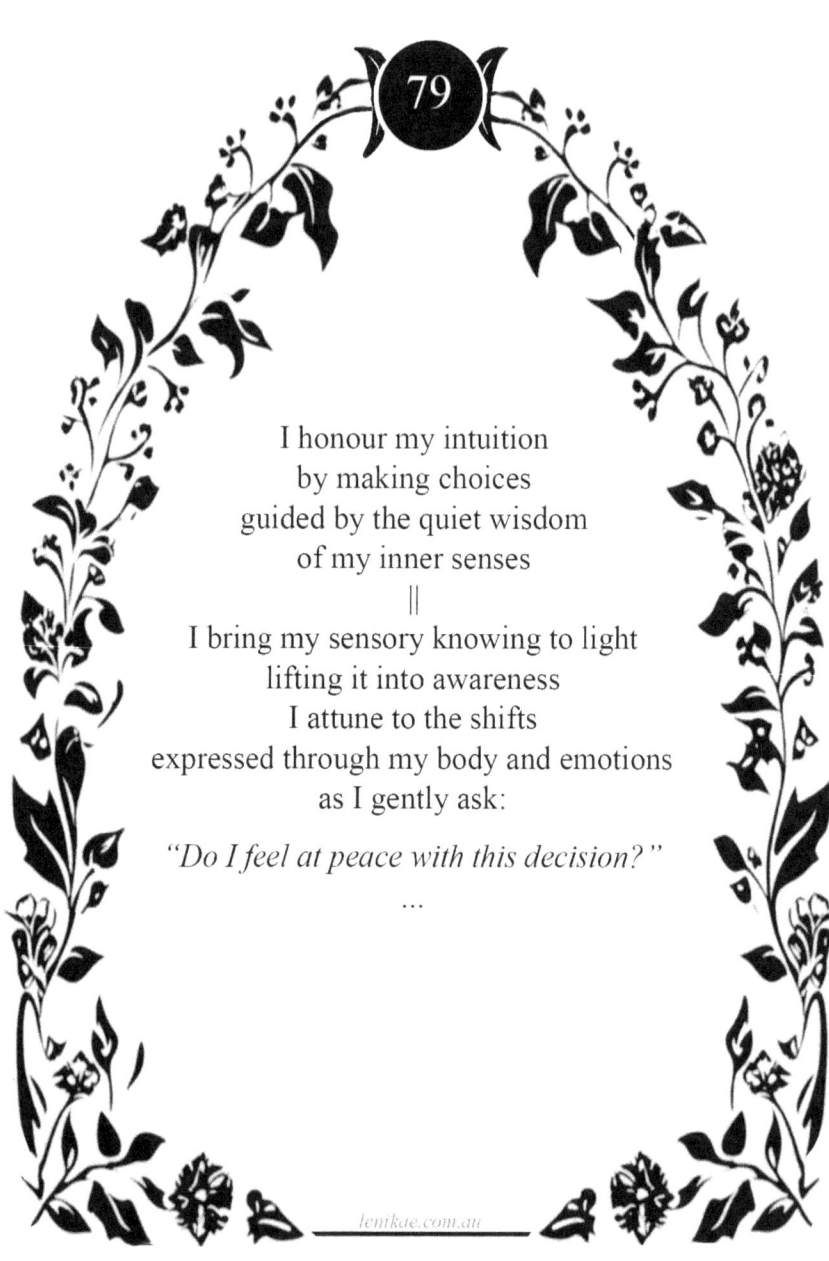

79

I honour my intuition
by making choices
guided by the quiet wisdom
of my inner senses

||

I bring my sensory knowing to light
lifting it into awareness
I attune to the shifts
expressed through my body and emotions
as I gently ask:

"Do I feel at peace with this decision?"

...

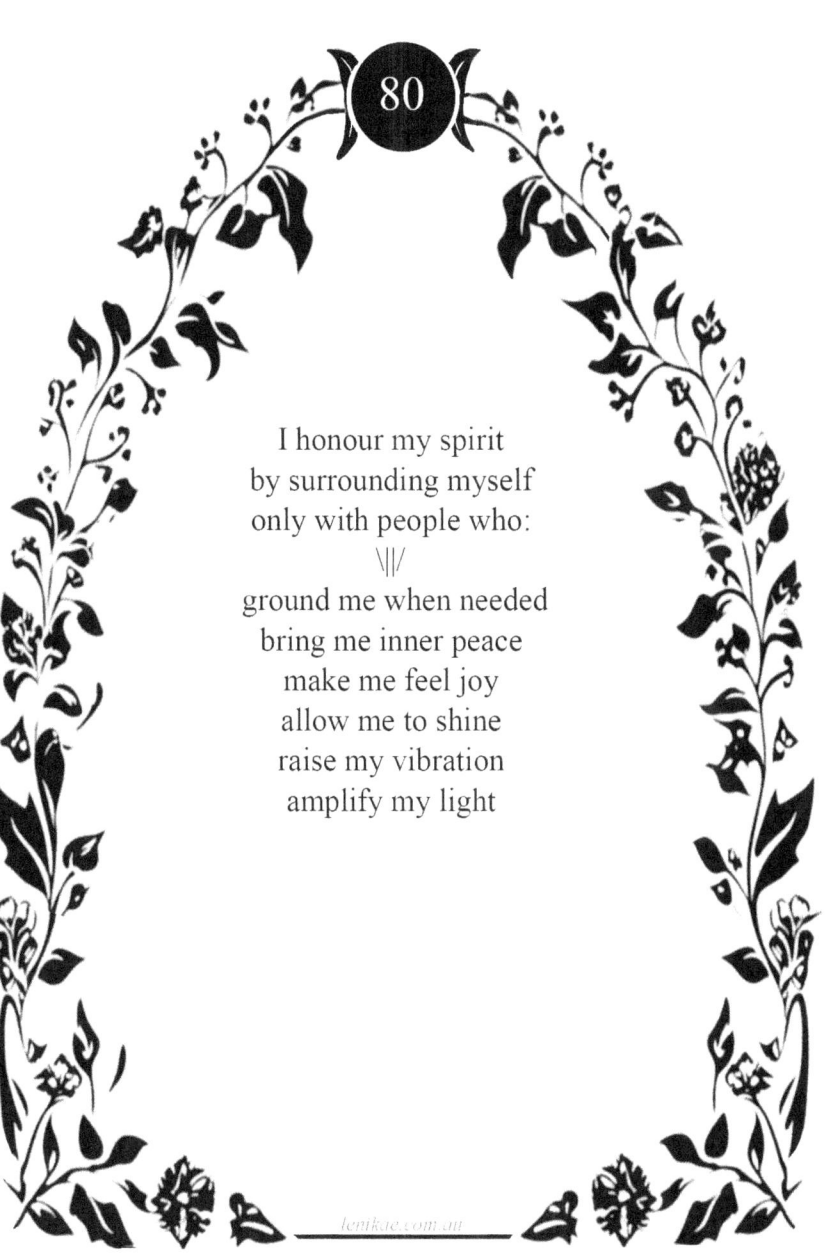

80

I honour my spirit
by surrounding myself
only with people who:
\|||/
ground me when needed
bring me inner peace
make me feel joy
allow me to shine
raise my vibration
amplify my light

81

I gift myself
permission to explore
to awaken to new possibilities
that light up my heart and bring me joy
I do this to honour my soul
/\
I am deserving
of a life that is full
\/
full of light
full of love
full of joy

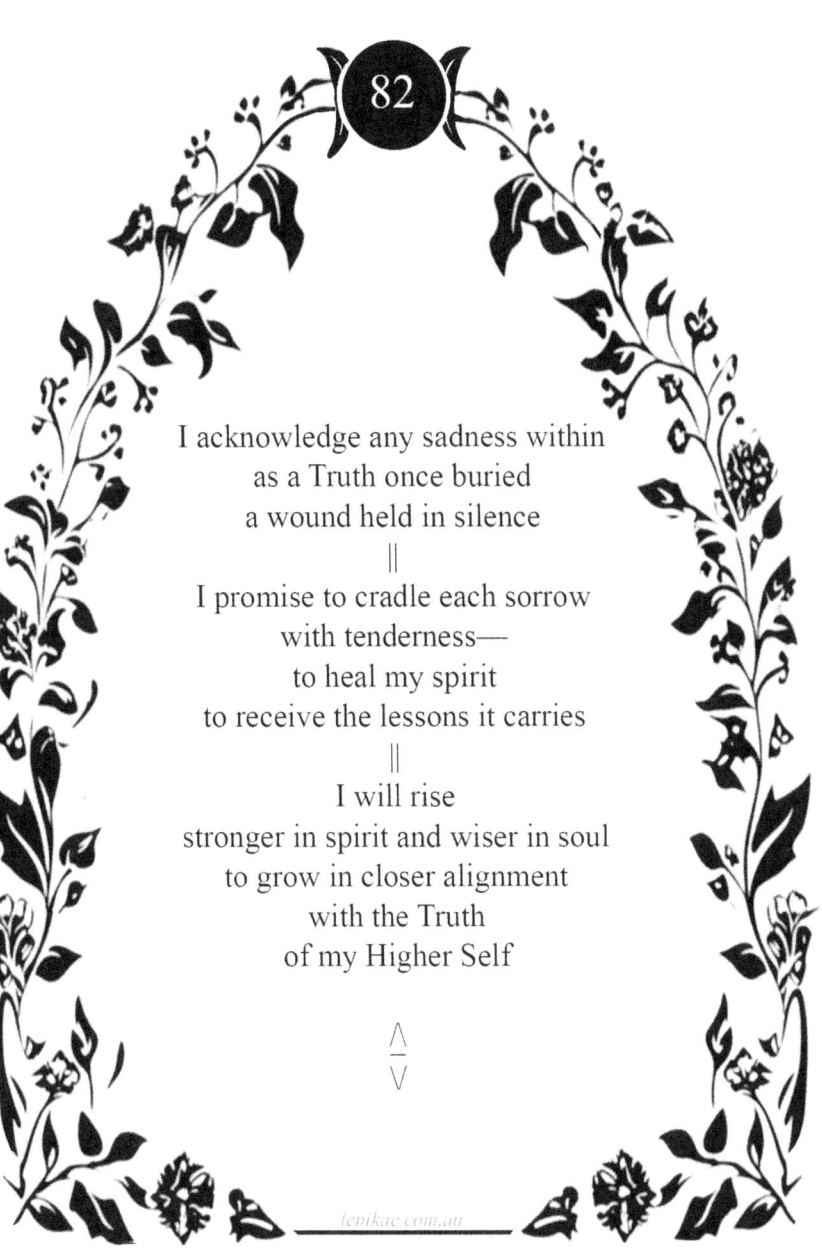

I acknowledge any sadness within
as a Truth once buried
a wound held in silence

||

I promise to cradle each sorrow
with tenderness—
to heal my spirit
to receive the lessons it carries

||

I will rise
stronger in spirit and wiser in soul
to grow in closer alignment
with the Truth
of my Higher Self

/\
–
\/

83

I am grateful
to my body, my temple
that holds the templates for my life
I honour you with good choices
with water, with minerals
with love
||
in gratitude
for my experience
for each breath
on this Earth

.
/|\

84

In the realm of dreams
I connect with infinite wisdom
I exist as a lucid, conscious creator
I am ready to embrace wisdom and Truth

85

Like the Sun
my light rises each day
reborn in spirit
radiant with love, vitality, purpose
ready to shine
||
to illuminate my world

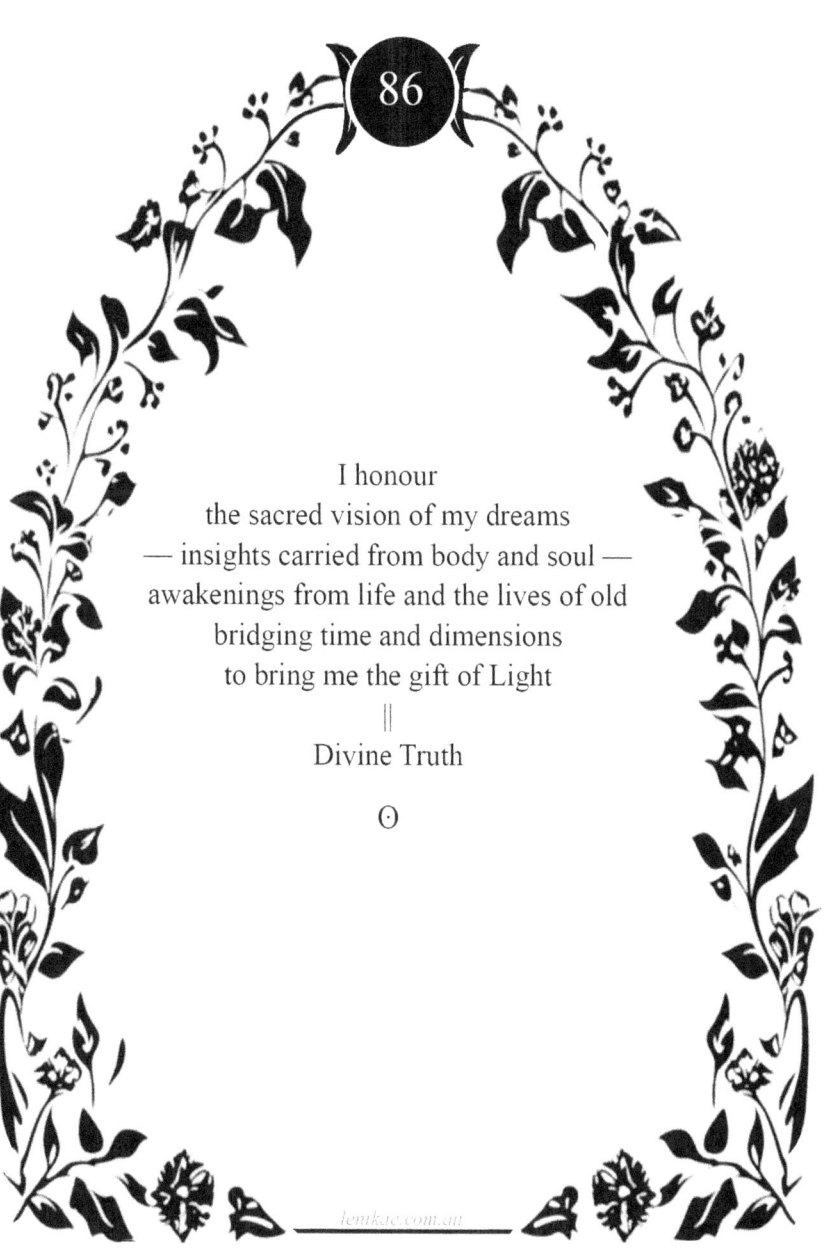

86

I honour
the sacred vision of my dreams
— insights carried from body and soul —
awakenings from life and the lives of old
bridging time and dimensions
to bring me the gift of Light

∥

Divine Truth

☉

87

Today
I take a gentle step
toward creating a more fulfilling path —
a life that honours
my heart
my soul
~~~
I am ready
to live the life
of my heart's true desires

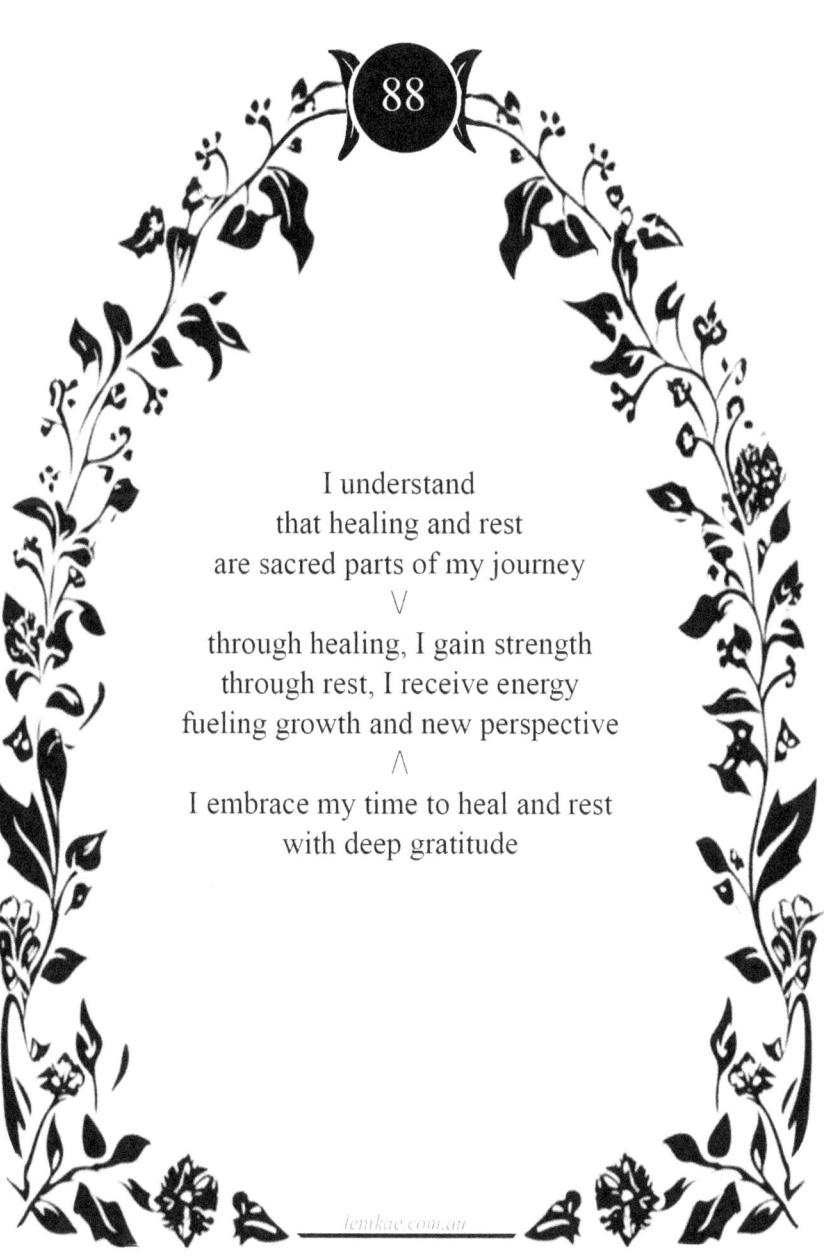

## 88

I understand
that healing and rest
are sacred parts of my journey
\/
through healing, I gain strength
through rest, I receive energy
fueling growth and new perspective
/\
I embrace my time to heal and rest
with deep gratitude

## 89

I will
be patient and kind with myself
for I am a child of the Universe—
born to this Earth
here to learn
to grow
/|\
to remember who I am

## 90

I gift love to you
— my inner child —
lifting you from shadows into the light
you are brave, strong and deserving
of a love that is eternal and bright

I give your wounds a warm embrace
then send them to the stars —
to weave a light that holds a space
to offer healing from afar

I wish you power over your shadows
may you always know your light
may your heart's flame dance forever
shining boldly, pure and bright

## 91

I stand
still in the NOW
within the limitless energy
of all there is

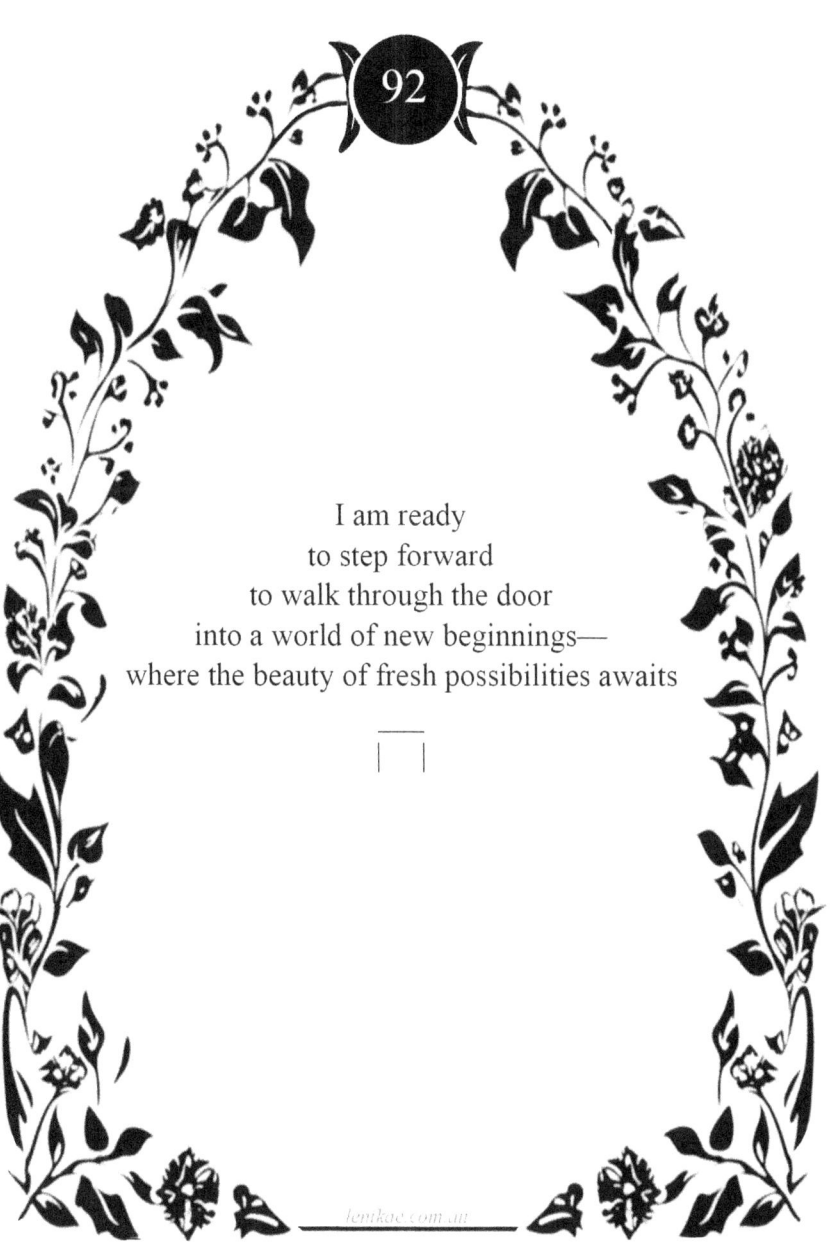

## 92

I am ready
to step forward
to walk through the door
into a world of new beginnings—
where the beauty of fresh possibilities awaits

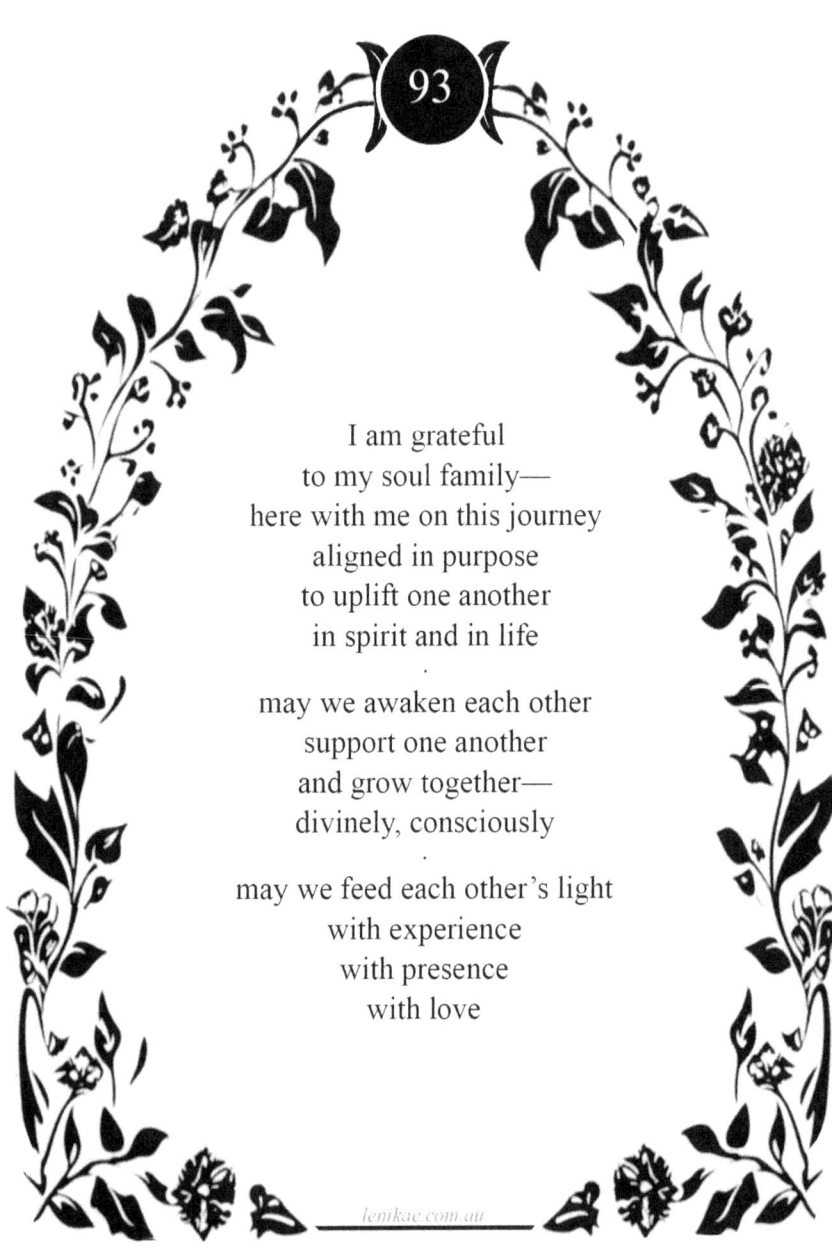

## 93

I am grateful
to my soul family—
here with me on this journey
aligned in purpose
to uplift one another
in spirit and in life
.
may we awaken each other
support one another
and grow together—
divinely, consciously
.
may we feed each other's light
with experience
with presence
with love

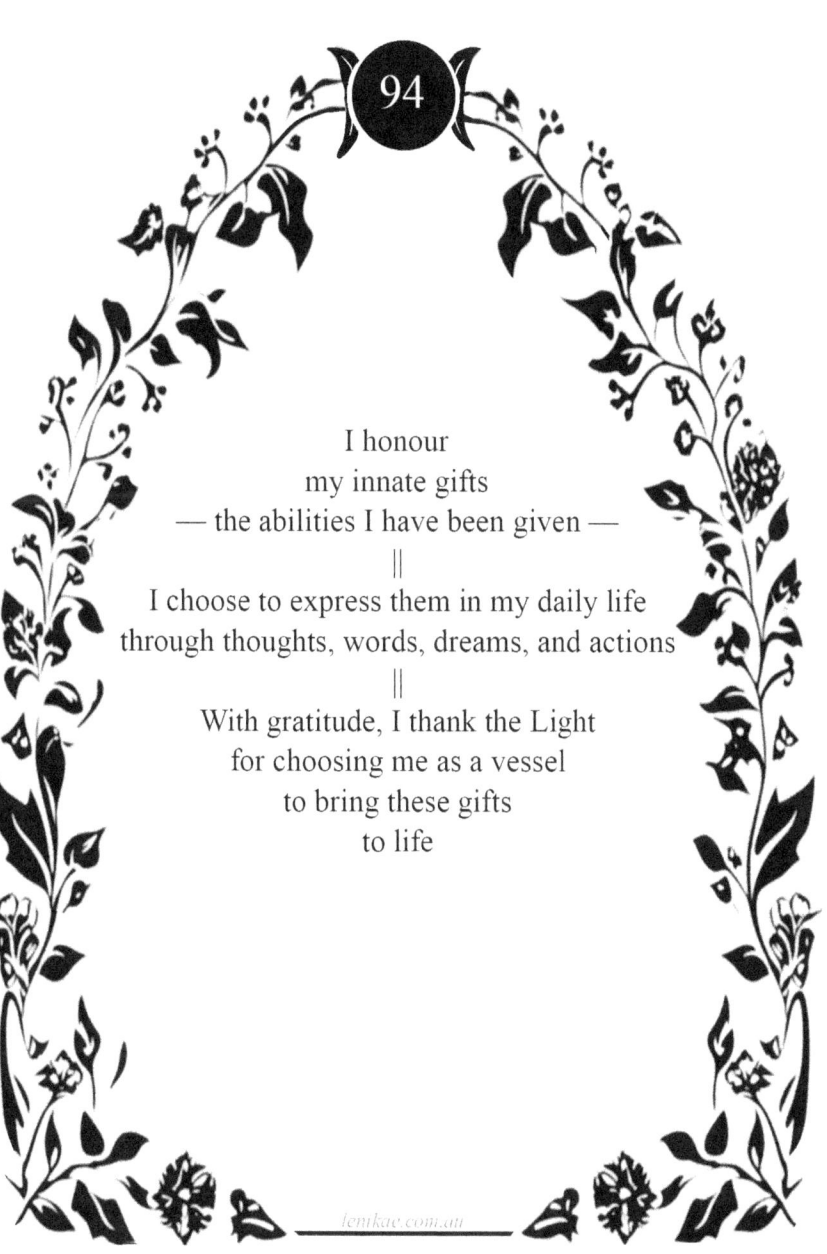

**94**

I honour
my innate gifts
— the abilities I have been given —
‖
I choose to express them in my daily life
through thoughts, words, dreams, and actions
‖
With gratitude, I thank the Light
for choosing me as a vessel
to bring these gifts
to life

## 95

I trust
that when the universe closes a door
its intention is to show me
that I am ready
for more

## 96

I honour the unique purpose
of every soul that enters my life
/|\
some are sent to show me kindness
some are here to show me love
some arrive as gentle guides—
like earth angels from above

some will teach me patience
some may test my will
some will make it clear to me
that I deserve better still
/|\
each, in their way, leads me
— in waking life or dreams at night —
awakening my heart and spirit
to my power
/|\
my Light

## 97

I send gratitude
to the Divine Father energy
embedded within the light of the Sun
the masculine force of action and activation
provider to all Divine creations
here and above
in life and love

O
|
V

## 98

I send gratitude
to the Divine Mother energy
embedded within nature, Earth, life —
the feminine light of all creation
the force of of Divine transformation
giver of life and love

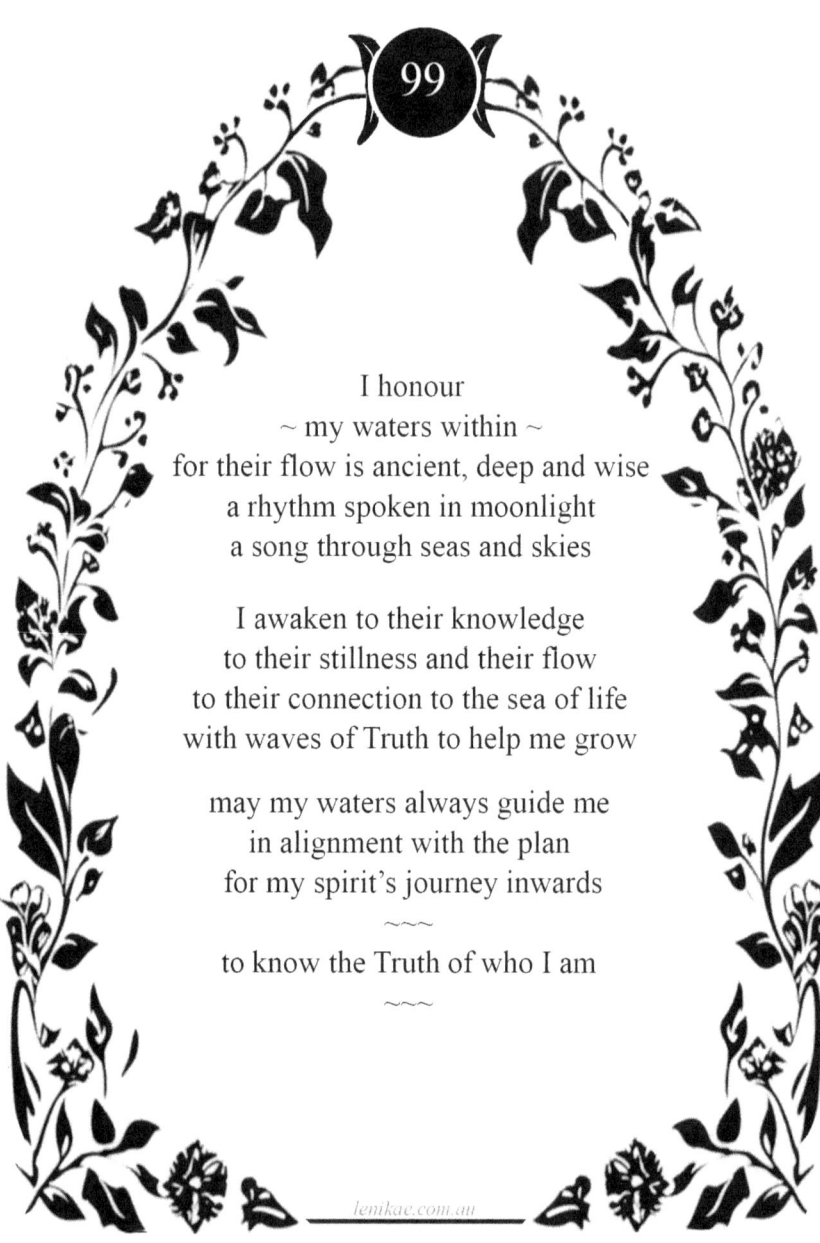

## 99

I honour
~ my waters within ~
for their flow is ancient, deep and wise
a rhythm spoken in moonlight
a song through seas and skies

I awaken to their knowledge
to their stillness and their flow
to their connection to the sea of life
with waves of Truth to help me grow

may my waters always guide me
in alignment with the plan
for my spirit's journey inwards

~~~

to know the Truth of who I am

~~~

100

I trust
in the Universe
to follow every ending
with a new gift for the soul —
just as the caterpillar
does not yet know
the beauty that
awaits

" Take note of life's whispers "

- Leni Kae

Notes

"There is always more — more to feel, to learn, to become."

— Leni Kae

A GIFT FROM THE AUTHOR

Download Your Free Printable Mantra Art Print:
www.lenikae.com.au/books

Visit lenikae.com.au to receive your FREE Printable Mantra Art Print—featuring an inspiring mantra and a beautiful line art drawing, lovingly created by Leni Kae.

Bring daily inspiration into your space and stay connected to the light within.

ABOUT THE AUTHOR

Leni Kae is a spiritual artist and intuitive writer from Sydney, Australia. Her visual and written works are deeply inspired by nature and its energy, exploring the profound connection between the natural world, the human spirit and the emotional landscape. Her creations are often channeled through meditation or dream states, allowing intuitive energy to guide the expression of messages meant to heal, inspire and awaken.

" The arts and nature are powerful companions on our journey of conscious awakening. They invite us to visit the concept of 'Unity' and see ourselves as part of a bigger universe."
~ Leni Kae

Qualifications: Certificate in Meditation Teaching | Certificate in Colour Therapy | Certificate in Educational Psychology | Postgraduate Certificate in Arts & Cultural Management (Deakin) | Bachelor of Commerce (UNSW)

ART BY LENI KAE

Leni Kae is a recognised finalist in numerous Australian art prizes. Her popular *Animal Spirit* series explores the energetic bond between humans and animals, with a focus on birds as symbols of freedom and intuition.

Your **FREE LINE ART GIFT** (page 126) is from Leni's *Lines* series — a collection of drawings and illustrations that explore the simplicity and beauty of line art as a way to guide focus and cultivate gratitude for life's simple joys.

Discover and Invest in Art by Leni Kae:
www.lenikae.com.au

Onine Galleries:
www.bluethumb.com.au/lenikae
www.artloversaustralia.com.au/artist/leni-kae

**JOIN LENI KAE ON INSTAGRAM
TAG YOUR ART OR FAVOURITE MANTRAS!**

@lenikae

MORE BOOKS BY LENI KAE ON AMAZON

https://amazon.com/author/leni-kae

" There is never truly an end –
just a movement
into something new. "

— Leni Kae

www.ingramcontent.com/pod-product-compliance
Lightning Source LLC
Chambersburg PA
CBHW071247070526
44583CB00017B/2363